BOOK THREE

The Take-Action Guide to

World Class
Learners

*This book is dedicated to helping schools and teachers
to transform their educational setting into a global campus so as
to enable the development of globally competent entrepreneurs.*

BOOK THREE

The Take-Action Guide to

World Class Learners

How to Create a
Campus Without Borders

Yong Zhao

Homa Tavangar • Emily McCarren

Gabriel F. Rshaid • Kay Tucker

CORWIN
A SAGE Publishing Company

FOR INFORMATION:

Corwin

A SAGE Company

2455 Teller Road

Thousand Oaks, California 91320

(800) 233-9936

www.corwin.com

SAGE Publications Ltd.

1 Oliver's Yard

55 City Road

London EC1Y 1SP

United Kingdom

SAGE Publications India Pvt. Ltd.

B 1/I 1 Mohan Cooperative Industrial Area

Mathura Road, New Delhi 110 044

India

SAGE Publications Asia-Pacific Pte. Ltd.

3 Church Street

#10-04 Samsung Hub

Singapore 049483

Executive Editor: Arnis Burvikovs

Associate Editor: Desirée A. Bartlett

Editorial Assistant: Andrew Olson

Production Editor: Amy Schroller

Copy Editor: Lana Todorovic-Arndt

Typesetter: C&M Digitals (P) Ltd.

Proofreader: Laura Webb

Indexer: Rick Hurd

Cover Designer: Rose Storey

Marketing Manager: Ann Mesick

Printed in the United States of America

Library of Congress Cataloging-in-Publication Data

Names: Zhao, Yong, 1965– author.

Title: The take-action guide to world class learners. Book 3, How to create a campus without borders / Yong Zhao, Homa Tavangar, Emily McCarren, Gabriel F. Rshaid, Kay Tucker.

Other titles: How to create a campus without borders

Description: Thousand Oaks, California. : Corwin, A SAGE Company, 2016. | Includes index.

Identifiers: LCCN 2015040354 | ISBN 978-1-4833-3954-2 (pbk. : alk. paper)

Subjects: LCSH: International education. | Education and globalization.

Classification: LCC LC1090 .Z43 2016 | DDC 370.116—dc23 LC record available at http://lccn.loc.gov/2015040354

This book is printed on acid-free paper.

Certified Chain of Custody
Promoting Sustainable Forestry
www.sfiprogram.org
SFI-01268

SFI label applies to text stock

16 17 18 19 20 10 9 8 7 6 5 4 3 2 1

Contents

About the Authors

 Yong Zhao currently serves as the presidential chair and director of the Institute for Global and Online Education in the College of Education, University of Oregon, where he is also a professor in the Department of Educational Measurement, Policy, and Leadership. He is also a professorial fellow at the Mitchell Institute for Health and Education Policy, Victoria University. His works focus on the implications of globalization and technology on education. He has published over 100 articles and 20 books, including *Who's Afraid of the Big Bad Dragon: Why China Has the Best (and Worst) Education System in the World*, *Catching Up or Leading the Way: American Education in the Age of Globalization* and *World Class Learners: Educating Creative and Entrepreneurial Students*. He is a recipient of the Early Career Award from the American Educational Research Association and was named one of the 2012 ten most influential people in educational technology by the *Tech & Learn Magazine*. He is an elected fellow of the International Academy for Education. His latest book *World Class Learners* has won several awards including the Society of Professors of Education Book Award (2013), Association of Education Publishers' (AEP) Judges' Award, and Distinguished Achievement Award in Education Leadership (2013).

Homa Sabet Tavangar is the author of *Growing Up Global: Raising Children to Be At Home in the World* and *The Global Education Toolkit for Elementary Learners,* and contributor to *Mastering Global Literacy* by Heidi Hayes-Jacobs. Homa's work is sparking initiatives to help audiences from CEOs to kindergartners learn and thrive in a global context—and have fun along the way. She is an education and cultural consultant to NBC TV on original programming; she is also a contributing writer for the *Huffington Post,* PBS, Momsrising, GOOD, Ashoka's Start Empathy, *National Geographic,* and Edutopia, among other media, and is a sought-after speaker and trainer around globalization and global citizenship, parenting, globalizing curriculum, empathy, diversity, and inclusion. Homa spent 20 years working in global competitiveness, organizational, business, and international development with hundreds of businesses, nonprofits, and public organizations, before turning her attention to global education. She speaks four languages, and her religious heritage includes four of the world's major faiths. Passionate around issues of opportunity and equality for women and girls, she has worked on these issues for private companies and the World Bank, and served on various nonprofit boards, including currently on the Board and Executive Committee of the Tahirih Justice Center, a national leader protecting immigrant women and girls fleeing violence. She is married and the mother of three daughters.

Emily McCarren is the high school principal at the Punahou School in Honolulu, Hawaii, the largest single campus K–12 independent school in the United States. Originally from Vermont, McCarren graduated from Colby College in Maine where she majored in Spanish and biology, and was a two-sport athlete, captaining the alpine ski team and lacrosse team. She holds two master's degrees: in Spanish Literature from the Saint Louis University's Madrid campus and in Educational Leadership from the Klingenstein Center at Teachers College, Columbia University. She is completing her PhD in educational technology at the University of Hawaii, where her dissertation examines the role of teacher care on a student's online learning experience. McCarren began her career teaching Spanish and geometry at Swiss Semester, a program for American students in the Swiss Alps. Next, she worked at The Thacher School in Ojai, California, where she taught, coached, and served as a residential advisor for 6 years before joining the faculty at the Punahou School in Honolulu, Hawaii, in 2006. At Punahou, she has taught all levels of Academy Spanish and a year of biology, served as a department head of both Asian-Pacific and European Languages, and as Academy Summer School director. McCarren was appointed to lead Punahou's Wo International Center in 2012, where she worked to broaden the global perspective of students and faculty while strengthening Punahou's role as a global educational leader.

Gabriel F. Rshaid is the headmaster of St. Andrew's Scots School in Buenos Aires, Argentina, the oldest bilingual school in the world, and a Professional Development Associate with the Leadership and Learning Center in Denver, Colorado. A former board member of ASCD, he is the author of the following books: *Learning for the Future: Rethinking Schools for the 21st Century*, *The 21st Century Classroom*, and *From Out of This World: Leadership and Life Lessons From the Space Program*. He has presented all over the world on the future of learning and 21st Century Education, as well as conducted numerous workshops, retreats, and seminars for educators and administrators.

Kay Tucker's vision and passion is to actively engage in defining and creating a culture for World Class Learning. She collaborates with educators to create ecosystems for sustainable learning including space, context, and technologies; designs and implements professional development opportunities; and originates systems and tools to impact change. As the World Class Education Specialist at Lone Tree Elementary in Douglas County, Colorado, she is in charge of creating a model of teaching and learning driven by current global educational reform and a World Class Education based on the thinking of Dr. Yong Zhao. In this model, students learn in an integrated manner as they align their strengths and passions in solving problems within a real-world context. In flexible environments, students navigate curriculum through inquiry and create their own learning pathways, while teachers facilitate opportunities, provide resources, and target teach on an as-needed basis. Kay Tucker's career in education spans 20 years. She has an undergraduate degree in fine arts from the University of Colorado Boulder and a master's degree in curriculum and instruction from the University of Colorado at Denver.

Introduction

Making World Class Learners

by Yong Zhao

No More Boomerang Kids

"One in five people in their 20s and early 30s is currently living with his or her parents," writes a 2014 *New York Times Magazine* article, "and 60 percent of all young adults receive financial support from them. That's a significant increase from a generation ago, when only one in 10 young adults moved back home and few received financial support." The article "It's Official: The Boomerang Kids Won't Leave" once again brought much attention to the issue of the economic conditions of today's youth, the boomerang generation. For many reasons, mostly the lack of financial resources to be independent, an increasing number of today's youth return to live with their parents, after briefly living away, mostly for pursuing higher education.

Gavin Newton Tanzer

There are of course exceptions. Gavin Newton Tanzer is one of them. Not only is he not returning to live with his parents, but he has been helping others to find hope and future in distant lands. A 25-year-old American living in China, Gavin has founded several companies and nonprofit organizations that help future youth become financially independent and socially responsible individuals in the globalized world. In 2010, while still a student at Columbia University, Gavin founded China Pathway, a company that provides consulting services for Chinese students intending to study abroad and Chinese educational institutions to develop study abroad pathway programs. In 2011, he founded Uexcel International Academy, with Compass Education Group, to bring international school programs to public schools in China. Both businesses have been profitable. He has dabbled in other businesses as well, including founding a company for data mining and even a company for movie production. "Neither of which went anywhere, but stemmed from what I saw as opportunities," said Gavin.

Gavin left home upon graduating from Newtown High School in 2007 at the age of 18. He spent a year in China, learning the language and culture, making friends, and honing his organizational skills by serving at the youth volunteer programs in the 2008 Beijing Olympic Games. He now speaks fluent Mandarin Chinese, with a Beijing accent, in addition to French and Spanish. More importantly, he spotted the need for a better understanding about China. When he returned to attend college at Columbia, he started the Global China Connection (GCC) student organization, which now boasts more than 60 chapters in over 10 countries. GCC connects thousands of future youth leaders who have a desire and are willing to have a better understanding of China and opportunities in China.

But most impressive is Gavin's new venture, which is transforming education in China. In 2012, he founded Sunrise International Education, a company that develops and provides extracurricular programs in China and ultimately globally. The premier program of Sunrise is the introduction of American-style high school debate in China. After only 2 years, Sunrise programs have trained nearly 100,000 Chinese students and organized tournaments with over 6,000 participants. "We are set to have around 12,000 in tournament this year [2014]," according to Gavin. And Sunrise is working on adding two more leagues: drama and business. In many ways, Gavin's programs are delivering more impact on Chinese students than many government reform efforts in terms of helping them develop critical thinking skills, communication and public speaking skills, and independent thinking skills, in addition to broadening their educational experiences. By the way, Gavin's company has over 20 employees, expecting to double that soon.

The Entrepreneurial Mindset

What makes Gavin different from the boomerang kids? The mindset. Gavin has an entrepreneurial mindset that makes him a creator of opportunities and jobs for himself and others. The boomerang kids have the employee mindset that makes them look for jobs that no longer exist. Technology and globalization have transformed our society. Machines and off-shoring have led to the disappearance of traditional middle-class jobs—jobs our education has been making our children ready for.

Since there are more boomerang kids than there are graduates like Gavin, it seems reasonable to say that Gavin is an accident, while the boomerang kids are the norm. In other words, the boomerang kids are the inevitable, while Gavin is a nice serendipity. This is because our traditional education, by design, produces employees rather than entrepreneurs. The challenge for educators today, if we wish to have fewer boomerang kids, is to figure out how to redesign our education to prepare entrepreneurs like Gavin so they do not happen by accident.

The Ideal School

That is the purpose of the book *World Class Learners: Educating Creative and Entrepreneurial Students*, which outlines a new design that would turn the Gavin accident into institutional arrangement. The design includes three elements:

1. *Personalization:* Changing education from imposing on students the same standardized content to enabling students to pursue their passion and strength through student voice and choice, a broad and flexible curriculum, and mentoring and advising.

2. *Product-oriented learning:* Changing pedagogy from just-in-case knowledge transmitting to just-in-time supporting of students' engagement in entrepreneurial activities aiming to produce authentic products and services.

3. *Globalized campus:* Expanding the educational setting from local, isolated, physical spaces to global and virtual spaces to help students develop global perspectives and global competencies.

These three elements form the basic framework of schooling aimed to cultivate globally competent, creative, and entrepreneurial talents needed today. They are about redesigning the three primary aspects of schooling: curriculum, pedagogy, and context (see Figure 1). The ideal school should provide opportunities and resources to enable students to personalize their educational experiences instead of receiving a uniform standardized, externally prescribed, education diet. That is, rather than imposing on all students the same knowledge and skills and expecting all students master them at the same pace, the school co-constructs a curriculum that follows the students' passions and enhances their strengths. In terms of pedagogy, teachers in the ideal school facilitate student development by supporting and guiding students through an authentic process of creating works that matter to others. To make this possible, the ideal school brings in global resources and engages students in activities that enable students to learn for and with students from all over the world. Simply put, the ideal school is no longer a physical campus.

Figure 1   Elements of Entrepreneur-Oriented Education

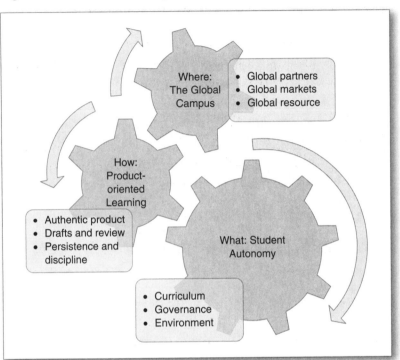

While the ideal school in the future is to have all three elements implemented, each element can be implemented separately. A school or teacher can choose to start working on one of the elements and expand to the other two. The elements can also be implemented at different levels depending on the context. An education system at the district, state, or national level can work at the system level to deliver any or all of the three elements. But a school can do this as well, with the understanding that it can be limited by system level constraints such as a state- or national-mandated curricula. Even individual teachers can implement the redesigned education in their classrooms, again with the understanding that they are constrained by system and school level factors such as teacher evaluation, mandated curriculum and assessment, as well as availability of resources.

Limited freedom to make changes in a school or classroom is not desirable, but it is better than maintaining the traditional paradigm. The ultimate goal is a complete transformation of schooling from employee-minded education to entrepreneur-minded education. But the realities of education today only allow for a gradual evolutionary approach to realizing this transformation. The fact that we cannot have the ideal version of the future right away should not stop us from acting on pieces of it. We can take baby steps before we leapfrog to the future. Thus all involved in education: policy makers, system-level leaders, school principals, and teachers all have a role, the capacity, and resources to make changes.

Making the Paradigm Shift: Books 1, 2, and 3

World Class Learners presents evidence for why we need the paradigm shift. It also outlines the basic components of the new paradigm as well as areas where we can begin the work. Since its publication in 2012, there has been growing demand for more practice-oriented guidance and support to help schools and teachers take on the task of transforming the outdated education paradigm. In response, we decided to work on three books, each addressing one of the elements of the new paradigm.

Three books are intended to be practical. In other words, *World Class Learners* is about the *why* and *what* of educational paradigm shift; these three books are about the *how* and *what* happens. They are cowritten by researchers and practitioners. They include specific strategies, practical advice, and stories of success and struggle. The strategies, advice, and stories were collected from classrooms and schools that have embarked on the transformation journey. They reflect both promises and challenges of the new paradigm when implemented in the current educational settings. While they are intended to guide and inspire, they are not meant to be prescriptive because each school and classroom has its unique opportunities and constraints.

The organization of the three books is similar. They start with a discussion of theories and definitions of each element, followed by specific suggestions for how each can be implemented and what challenges exist that may work against the implementation. The suggestions are specific to system leaders, school leaders, and classroom teachers. They are also made with the consideration of different realities—thinking (beginning), implementing (intermediate), and expanding (advanced).

Each of the three books addresses one element of the new paradigm. *Personalization and Student Autonomy* provides guidance and suggestions for actions that systems, schools, and classrooms can take to create more autonomy for students and enable them to personalize their educational experiences, to enhance their strengths, and to follow their passions. *Product-Oriented Learning* provides guidance and suggestions for systems, schools, and classrooms to design and develop infrastructures and resources to enable students to engage in authentic projects. *Globalized Campus* is to help schools and teachers develop global engagement activities for students.

1

The Global Campus

by Yong Zhao

THE GLOBAL CAMPUS: AN INTRODUCTION

This introductory chapter to the global campus will touch upon the following points: How is the global campus defined? How does the global campus fit in with personalized learning and product-oriented learning? How does a global campus cultivate the entrepreneurial spirit? What actions or attributes characterize students as contributing and responsible members of the global society? What are the various forms and shapes that global campuses can take on?

Once educators have reflected on these questions, they will also need to undergo certain mind shifts to implement global campuses: for example, rethink global competition; re-envision differences as strengths; adopt the glocalization mindset; and instead of the add-on mentality, implement the global campus while limiting increases in costs by rethinking all aspects of schooling including curriculum, organizational structure, infrastructure, staffing, and culture.

The Global Campus Defined

The global campus is one of the three elements of the entrepreneur-oriented education paradigm, together with *personalization* and *product-oriented learning*. The global campus suggests the transformation of the learning setting, from traditional physical classrooms to the globe, physically and virtually. It also suggests potential changes in how students are organized, from one group of same-aged students located at the same place to potentially project teams composed of students of various ages, backgrounds, and skill levels from different locations. Ultimately, the idea of the global campus is to transform defining schools as isolated local entities confined by physical facilities so as to enable students to learn for, with, and from anyone, wherever the learners or teachers are located.

The Global Campus in Relation to Personalized Learning and Product-Oriented Learning

The global campus is necessary for the implementation of the other two elements— *personalization* and *product-oriented learning*. In a related fashion, the implementation of the global campus, personalization, and product-oriented learning requires at least three things: utilizing the available (collective) resources of the global campus; utilizing the (collective) instructional resources of the global campus; and addressing an authentic (global) audience.

- Few schools have all the resources to truly personalize learning for each and every student. But if schools collaborate across political and geographical boundaries and *share resources*, together they can provide enough opportunities to meet the diverse needs of all students, enabling personalization.
- Local schools may have difficulty finding enough experts to support product-oriented learning, but if they *look for support from schools and institutions beyond their*

physical confinement, they will have much more success. For example, students working on certain projects may need the help of other students from different locations to serve as partners in supplying the necessary information or to contribute the unique components necessary to make the project a success.

- When students engage in product-oriented learning, they need an *authentic audience.* When all students begin to venture into personalized learning and product-oriented learning, they may exhaust local audiences and thus need to expand. Likewise, some projects may be of more value in distant lands and cultures than the immediate local community, making it necessary to look beyond the local "market" to find an audience actively interested in the product or project at hand.

Cultivating an Entrepreneurial Spirit

The global campus is essential to cultivating the entrepreneurial spirit in the age of globalization. To succeed, entrepreneurs need to have a global perspective, when looking for opportunities, developing new products and services, seeking partners and resources, and distributing their services and products. Entrepreneurs also need to develop cross-cultural competence to act on their global perspective so that they can gather information globally, working with partners globally, and understand their clients from different cultures. In a school that operates as a global campus, students have the opportunity to interact with their peers from other cultures constantly so they can build their global perspective and develop cross-cultural competence.

Characteristics of Contributing and Responsible Members of the Global Society

An ethical and responsible entrepreneur is a contributing and responsible member of the global society. Thus the global campus has the goal of providing opportunities for students to learn about and address global issues facing all human societies, such as sustainability, cultural conflicts, poverty and inequality, as well as exploitation and human rights abuses. The global campus is necessary for students to develop a deep sense of the interdependence and interconnectedness of human beings as well as the seriousness of global issues. It is also a venue for students to develop both a global and local identity: in other words, being both a member of a local community, a citizen of a nation, and someone with a deep concern for people in other places, with respect for other cultures and tolerance of differences.

The Various Forms and Shapes of Global Campuses

A global campus can take different forms and shapes. Today's technology enables people to interact with people and resources in distant lands. Many schools already take advantage of online courses and tutoring from different places. Examples abound of students working with their peers from a distance. Some schools have built partnerships with schools and institutions in other nations to send their students on study-abroad trips. Others have begun to establish physical campuses abroad. But the extent to which most schools have begun to transform their learning setting from local to global remains limited, not only inadequate to meet the needs of the new education paradigm, but also insufficient to take advantage of the capacity of technology for global connections.

A global campus is much more than adding a few global engagement programs, offering foreign language courses, or study-abroad trips. It is reimagining schools as global enterprises. In a global enterprise, staff is distributed globally, resources come from all over the world, and students (clients) can be anywhere. To build a global enterprise type of school requires mindset shift in a number of areas: global competition, differences as strength, the relationship between global and local, and availability of resources.

Global Competition

The first mindset shift needs to occur in the area of global competition. The popular mindset of global competition is driven by the mistaken conceptualization of global competition as a zero-sum game. That is, there are only a finite number of jobs. When they are taken by some, others will be left with none. Nations are thus led to find ways to protect their jobs from being offshored. In education, this translates into actions that produce higher test scores than others, which is perceived as the indicator of "global competitiveness." But the fact is, globalization creates a new market, new customers, and new opportunities for business. The number of jobs can expand, but it will depend on human ability to create products and services to meet the demands of new markets and customers.

Globalization presents an opportunity for global redistribution of talents, knowledge, and skills. Jobs requiring lower-level skills will be shipped to places where such skills are available at a lower price, forcing places with higher labor costs to come up with talents and skills not available at a cheaper price elsewhere. Thus, global competitiveness means different things in different locations. We cannot all win if the competition is only based on price. We must compete with qualitatively different skills and talents.

Thus, when building a global campus, we need to not think that we are making others more or less competitive than us or that we need to out-compete others. Instead, globally competent entrepreneurs should look for ways to differentiate themselves, find their strengths and the strengths of others to come up with solutions that meet the mutual needs of all.

Differences as Strengths

The second area that needs a mindset shift is how to deal with differences. Prior to massive globalization, human societies had been isolated from each other by geographical distances, physical boundaries, and political organizations. Taking history into account, human beings have been separated into isolated clans for a lot longer than we have been connected. As a result, distinct cultures, religions, and languages exist today. Although technology has made the physical distance disappear or much easier to cross, distance in culture, religion, and language remains large. These distances manifest themselves as vast differences in perspectives, values, attitudes, and behaviors.

Human beings are much more comfortable with similarity than differences. We tend to treat differences as a threat to our own values and often times consider them to be inferior at the same time. Differences can thus cause anxiety and lead to disputes and misunderstandings. However, in the globalized world, dealing with people from different cultural, religious, economic, linguistic, and political backgrounds is essential. Whether or not we agree with certain groups or individuals, we need to learn to interact positively with them if we are to succeed as players on the global playing field.

If we think of cultural differences from another perspective, we will find that differences can be sources of strength in cross-cultural relationships. People from different backgrounds necessarily bring to the table different worldviews and perspectives. Thus, someone from one culture may point out problems or identify new solutions that had not been considered in the other cultural context. Moreover, differences hold opportunities for the globally minded entrepreneur. What one doesn't have can be an unfilled need and thus an opportunity for those who possess the ability to create products and services that meet the need. Even bridging the differences creates a need for those interested in and capable of cross-cultural communications and cross-linguistic translations.

In turning locally defined schools into globally connected campuses, we are reimagining schools as places where students learn about differences that exist today and how those differences are, in fact, opportunities. Students on the global campus explore why differences exist, how they function and affect the world, how to resolve conflicts and contradictions, and what needs to be done to create a more peaceful world. Students also develop empathy at a global level and the ability to understand other people's perspectives and needs.

GLOBAL AND LOCAL

The traditional mindset of education is that schools are local. They are geographically bound, serving the local community. In the past, it was believed that students would work and live in that same locality as adults. Quite often, school staff also come from the local community. As a result, the curriculum and learning activities are oriented to serve local needs. There are of course a few exceptions. International schools that serve globally migrant communities are one example. However, even schools interested in globalization typically treat the global element as an additional and external element.

Part of the local mindset is the belief that global and local are two different things. The global is distant, different, and disposable when necessary. The local is intimate, familiar, and essential. On some occasions, the local mindset leads to conflicting views about a school's efforts to become more globalized. For example, some may argue that connecting globally may reduce the school's capacity for acting locally. Others may think global services divert resources away from serving local needs. Still others may think that globalized schools devalue the traditions of the local community and wither students' the cultural roots.

These concerns are real but not necessarily valid if we can adopt a new mindset. Perhaps the best way to describe the new mindset is the term *glocalization,* which is *globalization integrated locally.* This term captures the spirit of the new world we live in. On the one hand, with the disappearance of distance, we can say that our "local community" has expanded to encapsulate the globe, akin to the idea of the "global village." On the other hand, we all still lead a life in the physical world, under the influence of national political systems and local cultures. Global issues often have local manifestations. For example, public health is a global issue concerning everyone all over the world, but it means different things in different localities. Localness is also enhanced when viewed globally. In a sense, it is only against the global background that one's localness becomes salient. For example, Americans are Americans only when they are viewed in the context of other nationals. When everyone is American, their American-ness does not get noticed. This is why we "earthlings" get mentioned only in sci-fi works about denizens of other planets.

The mindset of glocalization brings the local community to the globe and the global world back into the local community. Schools adopting the glocalization mindset work hard to help students develop a deep understanding of their local communities in the context of the global world. They are simultaneously keenly aware of their local identity just as they understand their positions in the global community. They encourage students to address global problems in the local context. The glocalization school engages their students in activities that teach them about the value of their local identity to the broad global community and at the same time about how global issues are manifested locally. For instance, students from different parts of the world can all be working on solving the problem of environmental sustainability, but they would all do so in the context of their own particular community and local environmental assets, concerns, and needs. By interacting globally and sharing ideas while working on the same problem, students benefit from pulled resources, a diversity of thinking, and collaborative work.

COSTS AND RESOURCES

To change a traditional school into a global campus certainly involves costs and resources, especially when global programs are considered an add-on instead of being integrated into the school system as a whole. The dominant mindset about innovations in schools is one of addition. When schools desire or are asked to teach new skills and knowledge such as global competence or world languages, they typically add courses to the existing curricula. This certainly requires additional costs and resources.

However, the add-on mindset will not likely be sufficient for the massive changes required to prepare entirely different talents. When we need a paradigm shift, we need to rethink everything. That rethinking is about all aspects of the school—curriculum, organizational structure, infrastructure, staffing, resources, and culture. In other words, the school will be transformed into a different entity that operates radically from its previous manifestation. The transformed school may not require more resources to operate, but it offers the new kind of education we need.

To transform a traditional school into a global campus, we can start by reimagining the curriculum. As discussed in *World Class Learners* and Book 1 in this series, a personalized learning experience is desirable for all students. To be capable of offering a personalized education to all students, schools must become museums of learning opportunities. Thus courses are treated like exhibits in museum that has both a physical and online presence to students' access from anywhere. In other words, schools do not have to be the originators of all courses any more. Instead of limiting themselves to only the courses offered at their local school, students can learn from online courses, and they can form coalitions to co-construct and share courses and take advantage of free resources such as MOOCs, Wikipedia, or the Khan Academy; using online tools, they can learn from professionals in far-away places who can instruct them via video chats. Additionally, students can serve as mentors and instructors for each other across geographical boundaries.

We also need to reimagine the organization of schools. In the traditional paradigm, schools are organized around classes—one adult teaching a group of students of similar age. This is why class size has been a persistent issue of contention and why adding courses add costs. But if we begin to pursue personalized learning driven by students, we no longer need to organize students this way. We can think of students as self-driven autonomous museum visitors who choose to participate in learning activities that are available in and out of the school. Teachers change their roles. They are not instructors, but curators of learning opportunities. They do not have to know a foreign language in order to facilitate the learning of it.

Furthermore, when the school is transformed as a global enterprise, it does not rely on only local resources. A global enterprise operates globally. It serves a global community, which means a school can offer its special programs to students in other places. This can be a source of new revenue and resources. Similarly, a school can also bring in programs and courses from other places. A school does not have to own its entire staff either because it can hire part-time professionals as adjunct faculty from other places.

SUMMARY

This book is dedicated to helping schools and teachers to transform their educational setting into a global campus so as to enable the development of globally competent entrepreneurs. Such transformation requires a significant shift in mindsets. It requires us to reimagine all aspects of schools and schooling. It challenges our familiar concepts about what a school or a classroom looks like or what teaching and learning looks like. These are not easy challenges. Luckily we have pioneers in this area. Many innovative teachers and school leaders have risen to the challenge and started this transformation. The rest of the book gives examples of efforts to transform schools and classes into global learning environments and suggestions distilled from these examples.

2

The Global School

Others as Resources

by Emily McCarren

The Global Online Academy, International and Online

The Global Online Academy (GOA) is a consortium of independent schools that offers high-quality, learner-centered online courses for students of member schools. The number of member schools globally has grown from 10 in the first year to more than 60 (and counting) today. The GOA provides several opportunities to students: First, it gives them a chance to take courses that for various reasons (scheduling, the course is not offered at their school, etc.) they might not have been able to take. Michael Nachbar, the founding executive director of the consortium, describes the vision for the GOA: "There are lots of schools that are global—that have people from all over the world attending them.

What we are doing is creating learning environments for people to inter-act who are not just *from* all over the world, but are *living* all over the world." In addition to promoting rich student diversity, the GOA model allows increased faculty diversity. "Why should we limit the faculty in our schools by geography?" Nachbar asks. "To get the best opportunities to our students, we don't have to be constrained to just those who live in close proximity to our campuses." (M. Nachbar, personal communication, September, 2014). In both student body and faculty, the school can be truly global.

Meg Goldner-Rabinowitz is a teacher at Germantown Friends School in Philadelphia who taught a Media Studies course in the first year of the GOA. Teachers at member schools teach one or two GOA classes. Meg's class had students from her home school in Washington and other member schools all over the world. In an early assignment, Meg asked students to describe themselves with one image (not of themselves) and one sentence. The purpose of the assignment was to examine the power of images in shaping the understanding of complex phenomena. One of Meg's students was a Jordanian teenager Fakahr, who was studying at King's Academy in Amman, Jordan. Students posted their photos and captions on a discussion board in the online course space. For her photo, Fakahr chose a dramatic image of the Twin Towers in New York City on September 11, 2001, right after they were struck by airplanes. Smoke and flames are obscuring the New York skyline with the backdrop of a clear blue sky. She captioned the photo with one sentence and shared the photo with her classmates, who were spread all over the world: "My name is Fakahr, I am Muslim, and I am not a terrorist."

PRINCIPLES FOR LEVERAGING RESOURCES IN OTHERS

- Establish global networks to serve student learning
- Push beyond the limits of traditional schools
- Engage experts
- Develop trusting and caring collaborations
- Embrace diversity of educational environments
- Nurture partner school relationships and leverage networks

- Outsource the great at your school
- Rethink ownership of credit

Establish Global Networks to Serve Student Learning

While Fakahr's portrayal of her self-image in this online course is provocative and deeply memorable, the discussions that ensued following her post were even more remarkable. The students engaged in a safe and thoughtful discourse about stereotypes in the media in their various home locations. They were able to reflect and work to articulate their local realities to a global audience, something they would not have been able to do if the students had all lived in one place.

The geographic diversity in the GOA can be international, but a global campus can also be about highlighting and understanding regional differences within single countries, including the United States. In a Global Health course in the GOA, a student from a liberal community in Boston was stunned to hear the opinion of her classmates, who grew up in a more socially conservative community, on the topic of abortion. In her community, she had not been exposed to opposing viewpoints or beliefs about the issue in the same way she was in a course with students from other parts of the country. There are many questions and topics that geographic diversity brings to a conversation and classroom environment: What are the perceptions of Arabs in different regions of the United States? How do people in different communities feel about controversial topics such as abortion? The students can then examine what they noticed in local media that could contribute to those perceptions. Or, in a Global Health class, what are the local health realities that may impact how people think about a specific topic? How does the rate of teen pregnancy vary from place to place? In all of these questions, students are given the opportunity to deepen their thinking while practicing empathy and developing an appreciation for multiple perspectives.

These are learning experiences that cannot be replicated with the same intensity where all the students live in the same geographic

> What can't we do in a traditional classroom that we can do online?

location. Many of the first iterations of online learning environments, particularly in K–12 environments, seek to replicate what is done in a traditional classroom as schools and school systems look to online learning to answer questions of scale and efficiency: How can we get more content to more students leveraging technology? The Global Online Academy is asking a more interesting question: What can't we do in a traditional classroom that we can do online? They are getting some pretty interesting answers and by challenging and supporting member school faculty, they are crafting remarkably rich learning environments for students and educators.

Even if your school is not part of a consortium of schools teaching online courses, there are many ways in which teachers and educational leaders can begin to consider the rest of the world as resources in service of student learning. In addition to leveraging online learning in innovative and thoughtful ways, teachers and schools can seek out and cultivate more traditional partner school relationships and connect students through meaningful projects. Also, teachers can continually ask themselves: Is there someone out there who would be more effective than I am at supporting student learning in this moment? And then, they can reach out to them and ask for their help. Teachers can consider bringing experts into their classrooms via video conference or text-based communications. These are just some of the ways in which schools need to be looking globally to see others as resources in service to their students' learning.

Push Beyond the Limits of Traditional Schools

In the history of schools, students have been limited by the resources available locally: the expertise of the faculty, the classes offered, or the facilities at the school in which they are enrolled. Technology has played a massive role in creating opportunities for schools to expand how they think about access to and ownership of opportunities. This has been happening, in surprisingly quiet ways, in K–12 libraries that years ago were severely limited by space and budgets to acquire, house, and circulate all of the resources that larger research institutions enjoy. Although financial realities are still a limitation, most teachers and students don't even have a good sense of the rich databases and materials that they now have at their fingertips.

Schools have always been limited in what courses they can offer based on their size and the expertise of their faculty, not to mention curriculum requirements and standards. When educators begin to see their schools as a home base for learning, but not the totality of the learning opportunities, they can transform the reality for students. In this environment, a World Class Learner can develop characteristics of openness, willingness, and eagerness to learn in the world, not just in school. Learners will begin to see school as a way to connect, and not an impediment to connection. And they will have a comfort and pride in the fact that they will be learning from, with, and for people outside of the school and their immediate community, ultimately forming their global campus.

Engage Experts

If a school is truly engaged in student-driven learning, students will be seeking out experts in a huge diversity of fields, on an ongoing basis. In this new paradigm of schools, as learning is personalized and outcomes are based on high-quality products, teachers must not, and in fact cannot, be the experts in all of students' learning. This is a huge shift for teachers, but a shift whose time has come. In the past, teachers might have invited a local expert in a field to their school to interact with their students. Now, interaction with experts can be more frequent, personalized, and globalized. Students can engage the experts they need to do the work they're doing. And they do not need to be bound by time or geography. If you can't arrange a live conversation over the phone or video conference, you can exchange e-mails or communicate on Twitter and other social media. Students have the amazing opportunity to think of the experts in the field as people to interact with, and not just the creators of papers and books to read, or lectures to listen to online—although it is essential to get all you can from someone's documented and public work in advance to be respectful of their time.

Livy, an 11-year-old in Texas, has been fascinated by lemurs for years. To encourage her daughter's interests and develop her passions, Livy's mother nudged her to connect with one of the narrators of a film that Livy had seen, focusing on lemurs. The narrator is a world-renowned expert in lemurs, and Livy expressed her interest, and also asked whether the narrator ever gave lectures in Texas. The scientist replied almost instantly, and the two now hope they can connect someday soon over their shared passion. Schools that can leverage students' passions and interests and allow them to seek out experts to deepen their understanding will be amazed by the engagement and excitement that students bring to their work.

Develop Trusting and Caring Collaborations

Good schools are chock full of educators who care deeply about their students. As we move toward a paradigm in which we encourage our students to seek out others to learn from, this can be hard for those same caring teachers. We ask ourselves: How can others know what is best for my students? How can we trust other people, in many cases people who are not educators, to support student learning? In this, there is an element of faith—we cannot control how experts respond to our students' inquiries. What we can do is support our students to be effective communicators and make the case that they are worth speaking to.

On a larger scale, there are collaborations in which we turn over some or all of our students learning to other institutions.

These relationships require a great deal of trust. First, there must be a clear and mutual understanding of the mission and vision, and of the reality of a student's learning experience in that environment. The most common way that schools experience this is through study-abroad programs. Programs such as School Year Abroad, which provides programs for students in China, Spain, France, and Italy and was founded in 1964, has developed a reputation as an exceptionally high-quality experience for high school students. Some of the sense of trust inculcated by School Year Abroad (SYA) is due to the similarity between the programs at many high schools and the program of study at SYA. Students in the program live with host families in the country and take most of their classes in the language spoken locally, but they take those classes with other (mostly) American high school students, and with little exception, the students take a course of study remarkably similar to what they would take in their school back home. This program has given thousands of students the opportunity to spend a year of their high school career in another country, which is a great first step. Still, as we move forward with our notion of schools without boundaries and global campuses, schools need to continue to grow their sense of how we can leverage the resources beyond our school walls in service of our students' education.

Embrace Diversity of Educational Environments

As schools explore and celebrate diversity of race, socioeconomic status, gender, and sexual orientation, they can also be considering assumptions about the diversity of educational environments. The top schools in the world have surprisingly low tolerance for academic diversity. While the course of study of high school students all over the world looks remarkably similar, transferring credits between schools, or converting real-world learning experiences into credit that moves students toward graduation or some sort of credential is surprisingly difficult. While there are regional differences, and great variation in nomenclature of year level and courses, there are certainly more similarities than differences in the content students study around the world. In spite of that, schools are surprisingly inflexible about student mobility between programs globally.

International Baccalaureate and other standardized curriculums offer some level of interchangeability in which students are able to move between schools with a certain amount of ease, but this is not exactly the vision here. The question is not how to find a standardized curriculum that meets all of our needs. Rather, we have to ask how we can allow students, in collaboration with their teachers and mentors, to create a series of experiences personalized in a global context? And one key to answering that question is for schools to be flexible in determining the boundaries of what counts as school and what bodies, organizations, or institutions have the ability to oversee that time. Schools have long considered themselves to have a monopoly on teaching and learning, and while there is still a monopoly on credentialing, if schools are to remain relevant, they will need to become more interdependent globally, and allow non-school enterprises—such as professional organizations, nongovernmental organizations, and in some situations, businesses—to be seen as places where our students' work can help them make progress toward their learning goals.

> The question is not how to find a standardized curriculum that meets all of our needs. Rather, we have to ask how we can allow students, in collaboration with their teachers and mentors, to create a series of experiences personalized in a global context?

To realize these aspirations for our students, institutions and schools need to create affiliations and networks that can support students beyond those enrolled at each of our schools.

Nurture Partner School Relationships and Leverage Networks

In the last several years, consortiums of online learning similar to the GOA have been developed all over the world, seeking to do together what individual schools are unable to do alone. These consortiums create a trusted network for students and teachers. These consortiums are a great step toward the goal of having your school be unbound by the classroom walls. In addition to these networks that provide opportunities for students, teachers should be creating global networks so that they have access to a global community of learners that they can leverage to support student learning.

Partner schools, sister schools, school twinning: Each of these terms can mean a loose or strong association with another school in service of student learning. These agreements have often been used for international collaborations between schools and range from program specific and extremely detailed (and sometimes legal) agreements to broad strokes language stating that the schools share a common mission or vision and hope to collaborate whenever possible. In some regions and countries, such as China, schools need to have official partner school agreements for students and teachers to be able secure visas for international travel. Some schools collect partner school agreements like trophies, but don't really do much to use the relationships to further student learning. Still, after checking with school administrators, teachers can do this work without waiting for the schools to establish formal relationships. There are many online communities that teachers can use to connect their classrooms globally (Hello Little World Skypers, the Skype for Education Community, and Flat Connections, to name a few).

The most effective partner school agreements are those established between schools that share a vision and philosophy and in which the two (or more) schools really work together to establish meaningful learning environments for their students collaboratively. This is not easy work and requires that people at each school are spending time communicating (with all the linguistic, social, political, and cultural challenges that can accompany that work). Also, partners need to work to ensure that both sides feel they are collaborators in leading student learning, and not just service providers to each other. For example, the Punahou School in

Honolulu, Hawaii, has a long history of international partnerships that (since the early 1990s) have been supported by
the branch of the school known as the Wo International
Center. This center does the work of maintaining the school's
various partner school relationships globally and coordinating the global education initiatives K–12. This involves
communication, coordinating visits of administrators, teachers,
and students, and also planning and implementing the
shared programs.

Outsource the Great at Your School

Another thing that schools can consider is what we are asking students to consider in an entrepreneurial, personalized
learning environment: What are the skills and talents that
our school community has that might be of interest to the
rest of the world? Maybe your school has an exceptional
English Language Learners (ELL or ESL) program. If so,
perhaps you could find a way to use vacation and summer
months to offer programs for students from other countries
to come and be in residence at your school to practice their
English. Or perhaps your school has an outstanding outdoor education program: You could invite other schools to
be guests, or offer to run camping trips for partner schools
over their breaks. These kinds of open-door policies and the
notion of looking at yourself as a service provider to others
can be of benefit to the school in a number of ways. First, if
your school provides excellent programs for other students,
it will become a fertile ground for cultivating partner school
relationships—schools are eager to connect their students
to wonderful experiences around the world. Second, even
if you are not looking at it as partner school development, if
you figure out how to market the opportunities to a global
audience, and include your own students in the program,
you will be creating a locally based global experience for
your students just by having students from around the
world participating. Finally, all schools can use additional

Ideal

revenue, and in some cases, the excellence of your school can be a valuable commodity to others, bringing in funds to support the educational mission of your school.

If we want to create global campuses for our students, we must create opportunities for them to attend schools, or have internships, or engage in learning that may not fit into the comfortable boxes that most schools have created. Boundaries of requirements, schedules, or curriculum will need to be points for negotiation. If we acknowledge that all students are on their own learning journey, sometimes at their own pace, and often in their own space, then we must challenge our schools to see concepts that tend to define progression in schools in new ways. How might your school respond if a student were to take a year of high school to study stress in schools? And what if our lemur lover decided that instead of waiting for this expert to come to Texas, she and her family were going to go to a wildlife conference to hear all of the latest research on lemurs and consult with a wildlife biologist at a national zoo to create up-to-date lessons for other children like her? When schools start to consider the resources available in their global campus, the possibilities begin to grow, and the barriers to learning begin to crumble.

Rethink Ownership of Credit

This speaks to another hallmark of the idea of global entities as resources for our students: humility and flexibility about what credit means in school. There is no grade level that is immune from this discussion. Starting as early as kindergarten, there is a deeply ingrained fear in many educators that time away from the classroom is detrimental to cognitive development. Schools have strict absence policies, many of which will require a student to repeat a course or a grade level because he or she was not in the chair for the prescribed number of days. Taken to extremes, this is absurd. Promotion in schools should be about demonstrated abilities and competencies, successful production of products, and meaningful rigorous work, not about seat time. If a student can miss a full year of school and still demonstrate that he or she was making a meaningful impact on the world in a way that aligns with the school's mission and vision, why should we worry about student attendance?

This is not to say that the role of school or teachers' relationships with students is superfluous. Students' learning should be meaningful and rigorous. The difference in this paradigm is the mindset that students' learning opportunities begin—not end—at school.

STRATEGIES FOR LEVERAGING RESOURCES IN OTHERS

Following are some additional ways in which you can improve the learning environments of your students to leverage resources outside of the traditional school system for their learning and development as a World Class Learner.

In the Classroom

Try out Mystery Skype (Beginner)

Using the Mystery Skype website, connect with another educator interested in a short-term online exchange and invite the world into your classroom in a low-stakes and engaging way. A classic Mystery Skype session is 20 minutes to an hour, and all you need is a device connected to the Internet. Even with just a smartphone connected to Wi-Fi, you can bring another class to your students. The purpose of Mystery Skype is to have the two groups of students determine where on earth the other group of students is through a series of yes-and-no questions. Depending on the age of your students, you can adjust the expectations of the exchange to make it more challenging and deep, or something that can be accomplished in a short period of time with little cognitive effort—but still lots of fun!

Include First Person Resources in
Assignment Expectations (Beginner-Intermediate)

Establish expectations in your classroom that students will not just seek out appropriate resources online or in traditional realms, but will have access to great thinkers. When they ask a question about a topic in which you are not an expert, invite them to reach out to experts in e-mails, tweets, phone calls, or letters. When they are reading the work of a living author, invite them to reach out to them. If they have a question about a political issue, have them contact government officials to gain a deeper understanding. In a classroom where this external facing inquiry is an expectation, you can imagine students feeling like the boundaries of school are not the walls of the classroom.

Explore Media Literacy and
"Ungoogleable" Questions (Intermediate-Advanced)

In thinking about others as resources, engage your students in conversations or activities about the value of learning from other people. This conversation is an excellent opportunity to explore essential issues of media literacy. Who is the author of a source? What is their credibility—how do you know if they are credible or not? How do we determine expertise? What are the ways in which connecting to people, and not just their work, would be a valuable thing for the students? There are many ideas and lesson plans online about ungoogleable questions and how to make them a part of students' learning experience.

Leverage Connections to Networks of Like-Minded Educators

Hello Little World Skypers is a global community of educators eager to connect their classrooms. Anne Martinson, an ICT teacher in rural Victoria, Australia, describes the ways in which she has used connections to help her students understand global diversity. Many of Anne's students from the lush farmland of rural Victoria have never even made the 4-hour journey south to Melbourne, much less traveled internationally—but thanks to Martinson's commitment to seeing the world as resources for her students' learning, they now have productive friendships and connections with students in Malaysia and Israel, having collaborated on a variety of global projects.

Be Reflective About Your Role as Teacher/Lead Learner (Beginner-Advanced)

How do you respond when you don't know the answer to questions your students ask? How often is it even possible in your class for your students to ask questions that you don't know the answer to? For a week, keep track of the questions that your students ask and how you respond. Have a partner faculty member come to your class and document the questions and answers in your class like an anthropologist: Who asks? Who answers? What does the flow of ideas look like in your class? Then, in a second week, think hard about the small and large opportunities to flatten the walls of your classroom and look for answers on the outside.

This strategy can start small and move into the very advanced stages. You can start by creating space in your curriculum to explore things you don't know about. Give your students space to lead by exploring something that they are passionate about and invite them to reach out to experts and develop their own unique expertise.

In the School or School District

Establish an Entrepreneurship Mentoring Program (Beginner-Advanced)

Establish or support a program that brings entrepreneurs from the community into the school to support and consult on student work. This could be accomplished through the alumni network or the local chamber of commerce or other business organizations. Experienced entrepreneurs tend to be eager to support students. Also, they are energized by schools making shifts that they recognize would have supported them better while they were in school.

Offer Collaboratively Designed Courses (Advanced)

The opportunities for like-minded schools to connect and collaborate on offering classes to their students are many. For example, consider two teachers running projects between their classrooms; perhaps they find that they work so well together, and the student experience is so rich, that they decide they will co-teach a course from each of their schools. Or perhaps two small schools collaborate to offer courses they value, but do not get sufficient enrollment at either one of schools; advanced mathematics or world language courses in high schools would be a likely fit for this.

Facilitate Studying Abroad (Beginning-Advanced)

There are small and large ways that schools and districts can encourage students to study abroad. First, schools can plant the idea of studying abroad with the simple act of posting flyers for organizations such as School Year Abroad or other organizations run by local, national, and international organizations. Offer training and/or travel to program sites to help counselors understand the opportunities available and encourage them to be supportive when students inquire about these opportunities. Also, districts can give schools the flexibility to be creative when interpreting credits received, courses taken, and experiences from abroad.

For example, if a student does an internship at a perfume factory in France, invite the school to consider how that might count as credit—could it be an elective credit in the French Language Department, could it be a chemistry credit with some supplementary lab time with a teacher? Could it be an interdisciplinary course self-designed by the student with outcomes approved by a committee of teachers and fellow students? Districts can send the message that these experiences are valued by highlighting the opportunities and celebrating and honoring students' learning when they return from their time abroad.

Educator Exchange Programs (Advanced)

The Wo International Center at Punahou School has a fellow-ship program that welcomes educators from other parts of the world for short-term (one to six months) residencies on the Punahou campus. These educators come from partner schools or other organizations globally and use the school as a lab for their learning and reflection. In return, the fellows provide rich opportunities for mentoring teachers and students in their areas of expertise, and teaching about and sharing their practices both as educators and citizens of other parts of the world.

Be a Resource to Others (Beginning-Advanced)

To internalize the notion of the global resources available to your school and/or district, spend some time thinking about the ways in which the excellence of your school or district can serve the learning needs of others globally (see the activities section of this chapter). What are the things that you do well that might serve the learning needs of other students around the world? As mentioned in the chapter, perhaps you have an excellent ELL program or an outdoor education experience that could be expanded to offer spaces to students from other schools. Or perhaps your district has a science fair or an art exhibit annually—what would it take to include projects or pieces from partner schools around the world? How would that expand the experience of your own students and those students from schools in other regions or countries? Also, how could your school be more inviting to students from abroad? Consider the policies and procedures for accepting international students and explore ways in which you might not only be more hospitable, accommodating, and welcoming, but would actually seek out international students to spend a term or a year at your school.

REFLECTION . . . WE CAN DO IT!

Beginning to see the world as a resource to your students can be a humbling but ultimately empowering journey. As educators, we want to offer the absolute best to our students, and particularly at successful well-respected schools, we tend to have a deep belief that that our school offers just that. However, it is now insufficient for schools to limit themselves to the resources, particularly the human resources, that are on their campuses. Teachers need to make a concerted and ongoing effort (and it is an effort) to flatten their classroom walls to both bring in experts and opportunities for their students. And going forward, the schools and school systems that thrive as world class will be those that see ways for their students' experiences to be broad, flexible, and open. They will be humble and eager to create a diverse slate of opportunities for their students and will refuse to be bound by the structures and limitations that have defined schools and schooling for so long.

ACTIVITY #1: INVENTING A GLOBAL CONSORTIUM

Participants: Teachers, students, and school administrators

Objective: This activity invites participants to build a global consortium that serves student learning. They will be invited to re-imagine the purpose of school and find hypothetical global partners to serve student learning. This 1-hour design process will walk teachers and school leaders through a process that breaks down their notion of what school is by examining assumptions about where knowledge is held. Having students involved helps the adults in the room unstick their thinking about teaching and learning and resist using some of the jargon that educators tend to use when talking about schooling. The purpose of this activity is to loosen up thinking about the boundaries of traditional schools and begin to see knowledge as held outside of the classroom walls.

Materials

- Sticky notes
- Permanent markers
- One set of 8x11 papers with the prompts: (1) "School should teach students to . . . "; (2) "In order to create our school we need . . ." for every four to five people in the group.

Process

Step 1 (5–10 minutes)

- Organize participants in mixed groups of four to five people (teachers, students, and school leaders).
- Have the groups post as many possible answers to the prompt "Schools should teach students to . . ." against a wall.
- Invite participants to be wild and think outside normal or conventional answers. Encourage them to say what they are writing as they post their sticky notes. Also, encourage them to build on the thinking of other group members by adding "Yes, and . . ." to the end of other thoughts.
- If groups seem stuck, or stop writing, invite them to think of the most illegal answer to the prompt, or the most expensive answer. Also, you can set a minimum number of posts per group to increase production.

Step 2 (20 minutes)

Ask each group to pick three to five of their favorite suggestions and have them begin to build a school around those things. Encourage them to think of the school as being unbound by the traditional constraints of schools and then have them discuss the resources that they would need to realize their vision. If necessary, have them brainstorm again (standing) with sticky notes.

Step 3 (20 minutes)

Have each group share their new school by listing the three to five things that their school will teach and describing (in no more than 2–3 minutes) how the school will leverage global resources to realize their vision.

Reflection: What are the large or small ways that some ideas we have heard here today could be implemented in our school now?

ACTIVITY #2: FINDING OUR IDEAL PARTNERS

Participants: Administrators, teachers, students

Objective: Other schools can be some of our greatest partners in developing our global campuses. In this activity, teachers and/or administrators will use the Internet to explore schools globally that might prove to be interesting partners. This is an activity aimed to expand awareness of the diversity of schools and potential partners globally.

Materials

- Internet access and digital tools for conducting Web searches
- An Internet ready device connected to a projector for sharing
- White boards for group note taking in Steps 1 and 3
- Sticky notes

Process

Step 1: Establishing What We Might Be Looking For (15–20 minutes)

As a large group (5–50 people) discuss the following questions:

What are the qualities of a meaningful partner school?

What are some possible ways that a partner school could further our own school community and help us establish our global campus?

What are some of the areas of opportunity for improvement in our school that we might look to a partner school to help us grow and evolve?

Step 2: Exploring and Finding Partners (20–30 minutes)

In groups of two or three, pick something that got your attention from the initial discussion, or something that someone in the group was thinking about but didn't share, and try to find schools that might be an interesting partner in that realm.

Use digital tools to look at the websites of schools globally.

- Leverage nation- and region-specific searches (advanced searches in Google). Use the Google Translate tool if the school webpage is not in a language you can read.
- Prepare a list of four schools to share with the group: Pull up the school websites and share (1) an interesting thing you learned about the school, (2) where it is located, and (3) why you think they might be an interesting partner.

Step 3: Share Out (20–30 minutes, depending on the size of the group)

Gather back together as a large group.

Roles

Timer: Each group has 90 seconds to share out (this is *not* long!). Have a timer and be strict.

Cartographer: Have one person put a bookmark in the locations of each of the schools in Google Maps or some other mapping tool. At the end of the presentation, you can share this map as a reference.

Reflection **(5 minutes)**

Pass out five sticky notes to each person. Have them write one (minimum) to five (maximum) sentences of reflection.

If necessary, use the following prompts:

Doing this activity made me feel. . . .

In this activity I learned . . .

This made me wonder . . .

Have the participants post them on the wall on the way out; if possible, serve snacks or beverages to keep people around to look over the reflection wall.

ACTIVITY #3: CLASSROOM CHALLENGE—CONNECTING TO EXPERTS

Participants: Teachers and students

Objective: The purpose of this quick activity is to help classroom teachers and students practice looking to external experts for help with their learning or projects. This can be done over the course of two or three class meetings to give time for responses.

Materials
- Internet access and digital tools for conducting Web searches
- Access to social media, e-mail, and other communication tools for students and teachers
- 3 x 5 cards

Process

Day 1

Step 1: Our Interests (3 minutes)

Have each person in the room write down an area of interest or curiosity. It can be something simple and common (soccer, the violin) or complex (string theory or sustainable tropical agriculture). Write the area of interest down on one side of the 3x5 cards.

Step 2: Defining Expertise (15–20 minutes)

Facilitate a discussion about what constitutes expertise. Use the areas of interest on the cards to spark conversation in addition to the following questions:

> Are there spectrums of expertise, or are you simply an expert or not an expert?
>
> Is anyone in the room an expert at something?
>
> How does the dictionary define expert?
>
> Are there any cases in which expertise is something you are born with?
>
> If you have expertise, can you always be of service to those who are seeking to learn? Why or why not?

Step 3: Pass Out the Cards and Find an Expert

Pass out the cards and make sure that each person gets a card that they didn't write. Ask them to individually do a Web search to find someone who is an expert on the topic on their card. Prepare a 1-minute (maximum) presentation on why the person is an expert in this field.

Invite one or two comments or questions after each presentation using one of the following the prompts:

> *I like. . .*
>
> *I noticed. . .*
>
> *I wonder. . .*

Day 2

Step 4 (30–60 minutes)

Give students the choice to either continue with the topic they received or investigate their own topic. Ask students to communicate with an expert on that topic. Have them plan out a communication with this expert after thinking about the following things:

What mode of communication will I use and why? Social media, e-mail, a written letter, a phone call, Skype, Google Hangout, Voxer?

What will the purpose of my communication be? To complement the expert, to ask a question? To ask them to Skype with the class?

Once they have planned their communication, they can send the tweet or e-mail or write the letter.

Follow up: For a week or so, keep checking in with the class to see what kinds of responses they are getting.

Modification: For a class of younger students (K–3), choose one topic and have the teacher manage the communications with the expert.

Refection

Lead students in a group discussion.

- What does it mean to be an expert? What are the requirements of expertise? Are they different for different topics?
- How might a broader range of people (beyond our teachers) contribute to our learning? Imagine some examples.
- How will I use this knowledge in the future?

RESOURCES

Global Online Academy. (n.d.). Retrieved from http://www.globalon lineacademy.org/

Hello little world skypers. (n.d.). Retrieved from https://sites .google.com/site/skypershello/

Lindsay, J. (n.d.). Flat connections. Retrieved from http://www .flatconnections.com/

Skype in the classroom. (n.d.). Retrieved from https://education .skype.com/

3

The Global Market

Others as Customers

by Kay Tucker

"Global problems as Enterprising Opportunities—Human beings face tremendous challenges: environmental degradation; drastic climate change; natural disasters; large and small conflicts among national, ethnic, and religious groups; hunger and poverty; energy; health; aging; migration; and unemployment, to name just a few. These challenges are global problems intensified by globalization. We could complain, we could criticize others for causing these problems, or we could try to look at them as opportunities waiting for the creative and entrepreneurial to come up with solutions. Being able to adopt a perspective that helps to examine these problems as rich opportunities for new products and services is what is needed for global business entrepreneurs."

—Zhao (2012, p. 223)

"What if happy meals resulted in happy kids and a happier, healthier world? What if students were able to grow them in schools? Our Green Bronx Machine (@greenBXmachine) is a non-profit dedicated to growing, re-using, resourcing and recycling our way into new and healthy ways of living. We're transforming landscapes and mindsets, harvesting hope and cultivating local talent while driving academic engagement and civic competencies in ways we've never imagined."

—Ritz (*Harvesting Hope*, 2013)

Featured Organization

The Green Bronx Machine, Bronx, NY

In his TedTalk titled *Green Bronx Machine: Growing Our Way Into a New Economy* (2012), Stephen Ritz describes how his vision of transforming a community with sustainable, healthy living options began with actual seeds in the classroom. In a classroom composed of a diverse mix of students—specials needs learners, English language learners, homeless, foster care, and adjudicated children—he challenged them with a "growing project." The students tended to the seeds, tasted what they harvested, reseeded, and grew even more vegetables to eat. In an inquiry-based and authentic learning environment, the students were intrinsically driven to be successful, so they often worked overtime—coming early or staying after school—to tend to their growing seeds. Another video, *Welcome to Green Bronx Machine* (2011) shows the success of their efforts as the students were able to organize and host a plentiful "Farmer's Market and Edible Plant Sale." Over time and with perseverance, the efforts of the students resulted in several thriving gardens of edible vegetables, and they went on to create what Ritz calls "the first edible wall in New York City" (*Welcome to Green Bronx Machine*, 2011). Word spread about this classroom project turned into a nonprofit organization employing students. The Green Bronx Machine eventually was contracted and paid to install edible walls in other communities.

Brendan Van Meter of Beaconhouse Media created yet another video called *Green Bronx Machine* (2014) where he captures not only the positive influence of Stephen Ritz as an educator, but the valuable impact of the entrepreneurial experiences for the students. Van Meter explains that after the filming of his award-winning video, the students continued to expand the business into a sustainable entity by growing their customer base.

> They have installed BOTH indoor and outdoor academic learning gardens that have transformed the entire community; . . . they've outfitted numerous schools across the Bronx and America! . . . The program is literally putting food on the table, putting people to work, inspiring students and teachers and changing destinies, lives and outcomes. (Van Meter, 2014)

Ritz is passionate about the fact that his students are literally growing their way into a new economy. The following is an excerpt from Ritz's biography on his Huffington Post blog site:

> GBM routinely generates enough produce to feed healthy meals to 450 students and trains the youngest nationally certified workforce in America. His students, traveling from Boston to Rockefeller Center to the Hamptons, earn living wages en route to graduation. Stephen . . . helped fund and create 2,200 youth jobs. ("Stephen Ritz Bio," 2015)

> In the poorest congressional district in America, where there is a high rate of concerning medical issues related to poor eating habits, and a high usage of food stamps, Stephen Ritz considers his students his "favorite crop." They now graduate from high school with solid academic competencies and a high sense of civic-mindedness, becoming healthy members of a greater community. This outcome is easily the greatest reward for all involved.

PRINCIPLES FOR SUCCESSFULLY CREATING PRODUCTS AND SERVICES THAT ARE NEEDED IN THE GLOBAL MARKET

What makes the Green Bronx Machine a success is that it incorporates many of the principles for success that are key when students create products or services needed in global markets and when considering others as customers. In this case, the entrepreneurial efforts of the students and staff created a product and service that includes the following main principles for success. The venture

- Addresses a crucial issue and need in a community
- Meets the specific local needs of a global issue
- Exemplifies social entrepreneurism that is sustainable
- Creates global experiences for students

Addresses a Crucial Issue and Need in a Community

In an area described by Stephen Ritz as one of the most expansive food deserts in America, the effect of poor eating habits was taking a toll on the residents of the South Bronx. The number of people suffering from obesity, asthma, and diabetes was especially high in this district where it was also difficult to find fresh food in local markets. Many students were unaware, not only of the benefits of eating healthy, but they did not know about the variety of vegetables and how they taste. These factors combined to create what could be considered as a crucial issue in this urban neighborhood.

This real-life scenario in New York needed real change, and because of this, it was naturally laden with potential customers. The people in the community needed more options for healthy eating—they basically needed more fruits and vegetables in their kitchens and on their plates. It was the reality of the impact of this negatively charged cause-and-effect situation that became the impetus for creating a viable product and service. This important social issue became a timely learning opportunity, and created the possibility for collaborative efforts between staff and students to establish and maintain a sustainable business with a solid customer base.

In a similar example, but one of a rural community instead of an urban community, students from Bertie, North Carolina, designed and built a structure to be used as a farmer's market. Their agricultural community—one that grows mainly tobacco, cotton, peanuts and soybeans—lacked access to affordable and quality food. In this case, the local community, the customers themselves, came up with the idea in conjunction with the students from their local high school.

> This past year, Pilloton and partner Matthew Miller led a class of high school students in designing and building a much-needed (and quite beautiful) farmer's market pavilion for the area. (Schwartz, 2011)

The tagline on the Facebook page of Windsor Super Market, where the farmer's market pavilion is located, now says: "Fresh produce. Fresh perspective" (Windsor Super Market, 2015). This is the essence of the positive impact that this venture has had on this community. It sums up in a few words how providing healthy food options to the customers is not only changing how they are eating, but is also promoting a healthier lifestyle in Bertie, North Carolina.

With a focus on product-oriented learning on a global stage, important issues within local communities are engaging topics for students to begin the process of deliberate problem solving leading to a product or service. Canvassing the community itself can lead to ideas for collaborative efforts. Analyzing cause and effect and the interconnectedness of systems and personal choices makes up the critical thinking that leads to a high level of understanding. If students understand how negative issues develop, they have taken the first step necessary to being able to develop solutions to the problems— and they have found their customers.

Meets the Specific Local Needs of a Global Issue

> [T]o be able to take advantage of the global market, entrepreneurs must understand local needs. They need to know what people need and what they can afford. Responsible entrepreneurs also know what productive products and services are to local people so they are not being exploited. (Zhao, 2012, p. 218)

Global issues impact communities around the world in disparate ways. To be successful in product-oriented learning, students need to understand the needs and wants of the specific community, or communities, to which they are providing a service or marketing a product. They need to understand the cause and effect relationship pertinent to the problem in order to create a marketable and viable solution.

Specific to the cause addressed by the students in these two examples, providing healthy food to all communities around the world is a challenge and leads to unhealthy living for different reasons. The United States Department of Agriculture (USDA) describes food deserts as:

> [U]rban neighborhoods and rural towns without ready access to fresh, healthy, and affordable food. Instead of supermarkets and grocery stores, these communities may have no food access or are served only by fast food restaurants and convenience stores that offer few healthy, affordable food options. (USDA, 2015)

The local problems associated with living in a food desert were very different for the two student groups, and therefore, they were addressed differently. In short, the global issue was addressed locally. The problem for the students in New York was a combination of several trends: an abundance of concrete (dearth of green space), an abundance of convenience stores, and a lack of gardens and grocery stores. The students solved the problem by using various methods and locations to grow and sell edible plants. They created edible walls and used container gardens to expand the availability of fresh produce for their community. They converted paved areas to community gardens and became involved in learning themselves and teaching others how to grow, what to grow, and where to grow. The community and students in North Carolina faced the same issue of living in a defined food desert, but their problem was almost directly opposite of the problem experienced in New York. Being an agricultural community, they had expanses of land capable of growing crops, but the majority of their crops were not of the "farm-to-table" variety. This combined with the extensive distance between homes and grocery stores to create their food desert situation. Building a solid weather-protected structure in which to house a local farmer's market was the key in bringing people together in one place, at one time, with the purpose of providing healthy produce.

There is value in addressing global issues on a local level, but there is also great value in expanding efforts to address these same issues beyond our local communities. This nurtures a sense of interconnectedness with others around the world and requires empathy and a deeper understanding of the needs of other communities. There are also many positive outcomes that result from understanding the commonalities of the human race. As local audiences are exhausted, students will benefit by using the knowledge gained from local experiences to expand to other communities or global markets. Some ventures may even be of more value going beyond the local market, but the caution is that a one-size-fits-all approach will not always work in expansion efforts. The diversity of climates, cultures, situational experiences, and so on creates a wealth of customers, but those customers have differing wants and needs. For every global issue—food crisis, water crisis, climate change, greater incidence of extreme weather, underemployment or unemployment, social and political instability, and so on.—there are distinct ramifications for the impacted populations based on place and circumstance. Even though communities may have similar needs, it may take a very different approach in order to implement an idea or to market a product. These are the variables that need to be investigated by students before they create new products or services for others in a global market, or adapt a current product or service.

Exemplifies Social Entrepreneurism That Is Sustainable

Social entrepreneurs are distinguished by the fact that their primary goal is to create social value and benefit, rather than to simply generate profit, however, this does not mean that social entrepreneurs cannot generate income by selling needed products or services. They can designate themselves as for-profit, or not-for-profit, enterprises. The Green Bronx Machine serves a dual purpose in its approach to entrepreneurism. Number one, they created the large-scale transformation from poor to healthy eating habits for the South Bronx and surrounding areas. This was primarily how they wanted to make a difference in the world. Number two, when they began to successfully sell their products and their services they generated profit. The money was not only reinvested into the business, but it was used to pay students for their work. The venture created paying jobs and entrepreneurial thinking opportunities in a community where most individuals would never think of starting a business. The fact that the cycle continues with a definite need, a viable product, a happy customer and a willing producer is what makes any business sustainable. What makes the achievements of the Green Bronx Machine so notable is that the social transformation continues to take place alongside a successful business model.

Social entrepreneurship always focuses on the transformational aspect as the primary driving force, but not all efforts need to involve money. Customers can still be considered and needs may still be met using other means and strategies. One effective way to approach this in the classroom is to consider students as reciprocal customers—trading what they know with each other. This arrangement of reciprocity has the potential of meeting mutual needs with students acting as mentors and instructors. An example of this in action is SEFOO,

> a global network of schools that are committed to engaging in student-centered, technology-driven, and collaborative learning. Students lead their own learning and contribute to that of others by designing and delivering authentic learning materials and programs for peers around the world. (SEFOO, 2015)

The intent of this network is simple—students help each other by sharing and teaching. They may help each other learn the language, culture, or geographic specialties from various locations around the world. They may collaboratively create a global glimpse of a topic. Individually, students increase their own knowledge and skill base as they create and provide information to each other on a collaborative global platform. Once again, the connectedness of the human spirit comes into play with common experiences. Students celebrate and thrive on the reciprocity of learning as they strengthen their ties to a greater community and a greater good. They are all each other's customers in learning, and in an ever-changing world, this process of learning will always be in great demand.

Creates Global Experiences for Students

As stated previously, the Green Bronx Machine exemplifies concern for the good of a greater community, but it also shows how a school can expand its boundaries and take on the philosophy of a global campus. This is a campus that considers the fact that there are others outside of their building and even their city that can benefit from their endeavors; there are others that will help further the thinking and problem-solving skills of their students; there is hope that any ventures of their students may expand and impact communities in other countries.

This venture meets the needs of both the students as clients of a school, and the customers in need of the provided product. It depicts valuable learning and skills development that can take place, both inside and outside of a classroom—experiences that are meaningful and resonate on a personal level with every student. As the students create the products and services, research and refine their ideas, interact with the customers, and maintain and grow their business, they are in a sustainable learning pattern. The students are satisfied customers of a school that is meeting the goals of education and preparing them for future careers or college experiences.

STRATEGIES FOR PARTICIPATING
IN GLOBAL MARKETS

In the Classroom

Spark Dialogue About What Is Working
or Not Working in Your Local Community

Why are things not working? Is there anything we can do about it? Teach skills and concepts and provide materials and frameworks that will help students understand they can be part of solving real-world problems.

- What do we know about the people we care about?
- What do we know about our local community?
- Who are potential customers?
- How can we help transform our own communities?

When we learn about each other and where we live, we have empathy toward each other, and that makes it easier to work together toward a common goal. Opportunities to create products and services become more visible.

Analyze Cause and Effect to Find Customers

Global issues impact communities around the world in disparate ways. To be successful in product-oriented learning, students need to understand the needs and wants of the specific community, or communities, to which they are providing a service or marketing a product. They need to understand the cause-and-effect relationship pertinent to the problem in order to create a marketable and viable solution and to find a customer base. Whenever students are considering a problem to solve, have them look carefully at both the cause and the effect.

- Analyze the Cause

  - Who or what is the cause of this situation?
  - Can we impact change with the cause? If so, how?

- Analyze the effect
  - ○ Who or what is being affected?
  - ○ Can we impact positive change with the effect?
  - ○ Is it possible to impact change with the affected? If so, how?

- Is there a causal chain?
  - ○ Are there multiple cause and effect happenings that lead to a final result?
  - ○ If so, how can impacting one of the steps influence the outcome?
  - ○ Who is being affected along the chain?

Help Create Global Connections
With Others as Purposeful Customers

The global stage should be a strong possibility for students to make a difference either from a civic-minded perspective or an innovative problem-solving perspective. How do we immerse our students in global experiences, help them create connections that will pique their curiosity, and help them find opportunities to impact change in the world? Expand the thinking of your students by bringing meaning and purpose to global connections, either as an entire class or for individual students. Ask your students if they have anything they could teach to others around the world? Are there things they could prepare and present to further the learning of others? Where would this be? Who would benefit? How can you collaborate to make this happen? Are there opportunities for reciprocal partnerships resulting in students as customers of each other? Consider the value of your students helping and being helped by other students, in the forms of sharing, teaching, or mentoring.

In the School

Be Alert to and Promote Expanded Opportunities Schoolwide

There is power in an entire school approaching a philosophy as a whole. Administrators and school leaders should be proactive in seeking out any possible connections for their students and teachers. Survey your community—go beyond the immediate stakeholders in the school. Expand your horizons initially by looking at connections within your local community and see how these connections could grow. The focus of this chapter is others as customers, but within the context of learning, imagine how this can play out specifically for your school. Be willing to plant an idea, grow it, and see what results in the form of opportunities for expansion of marketable ideas, products, and services.

During the 2011–2012 school year at Lone Tree Elementary, in Colorado, a leadership team initiated the idea of a school garden, where students could plant, grow, observe science, and see potential for entrepreneurial opportunities. Many schools were creating school gardens as an engaging place for students to be hands-on and learn about life science and healthy eating. A group of third-grade students and teachers took charge, and the garden was created with raised beds and an irrigation system. Over the next few years, the garden encountered many challenges. Seeds were planted in the spring, and over the summer, weeds overtook the garden and the plants often died due to a lack of attendance and care. In 2013–2014, the leadership team decided to approach the City of Lone Tree with the idea of collaborating to create a true community garden that would be sustainable and thrive throughout the summer months with active gardeners. The collaboration with the City of Lone Tree and the elementary school grew to include Denver Urban Gardens (DUG) who provided an incredible amount of resources, planning material, and guidance for the garden. During a planning session, the landscape designer met with all community members, including representatives from the school as well as students to brainstorm all of the elements wished for in the garden. A community garden committee has been established and together plans are moving forward with fundraising, and an expected planting date of May 2015. Plots will be rented out to active gardeners, and there are plots for the students and places around the garden for science and art integration as well as outside learning areas. There is an area dedicated as a farmer's market for students and community gardeners alike. Students have plans in place to sell seeds, flowers, herbs, and vegetables during carpool drop-off and pick-up times. Community members are now customers of this collaborative venture, and there are many opportunities for student-created businesses and a sharing of experiences and student-generated information via the garden website. Community gardeners will serve as school volunteers, sharing their expertise with the students. With a focus on how community gardens promote healthy eating, Denver Urban Gardens is a key resource with opportunities for students to connect with other student gardeners. This venture would not have been possible without school leaders seeking opportunities beyond school resources, and it has great potential to expand in so many ways with information, innovation and creativity. Follow their progress at the Lone Tree Elementary website, Growing and Learning in Community Gardens, at https://goo.gl/UFN28J.

Build Connections Into School Philosophy and Plan

Adopt a philosophy as an organization to promote global understanding. Create a plan for all students to engage in real-world global experiences to provoke understanding, thinking, and innovation. The Threshold School, a new school in Centennial, Colorado, opening for the 2015–2016 academic year, has a strong plan in place for students to be "thought leaders and change-makers." The school website declares, "Threshold School is not preparation for life. Rather, the years in Threshold *are* life. And life . . . will be extraordinary" (www.thresholdschool.org). With this in mind, they have scripted experiences for their students and opened up global possibilities for hands-on activities leading to action and understanding. All students participate in "large-scale highly collaborative undertakings" using a team approach and spanning time periods determined by the project, not the school day.

The Threshold School has schedules in place for experiential visits and have included these in their tuition costs.

For many schools and communities, funding is an issue; however, it is worth brainstorming other ways to reach the same goal. Planning optional experiential trips and using creative funding could be ways to offer similar global opportunities. If the physical movement of people is out of the question, consider how to create collaborative connections between global communities that could inspire the same kind of thinking and creative problem solving.

In the School System

Create Global Reciprocal Opportunities for Professional Development

Any school system benefits from strong school leadership and leaders who seek out and embrace new vision for education. In the case of creating and being part of global markets, system leaders should consider promoting and organizing trips for their school leadership and teacher leaders. These trips should provide opportunities to observe innovative approaches to teaching and learning as it takes place in actual buildings during real school days. There are many options to pick from based on a specific paradigm shift, or desired direction. Being able to see and interact with students and teachers engaged in daily activities is one of the most inspiring courses of action in order to drive change. Also to be considered is the reciprocal opportunity. What do some of the schools in your system have to offer? Would it be possible to arrange opportunities with schools in another part of the world where teachers exchange work time as well as ideas?

Seek Out Actual Opportunities for the Global Exchange of Ideas, Products, and Services

How great would it be to eventually see, as common practice, groups of students traveling with their teachers to other countries, specifically to partake in school days with the purpose of teaching and learning alongside others around the world? Could your district or school system, orchestrate opportunities to swop groups of teachers and student leaders as a means of exchanging ideas, practices, and possibly products, to meet the needs of others? The specifics of this might be challenging, but the resulting collaborative efforts would be powerful.

If the logistics of actual travel are too challenging, start with seeking out opportunities via digital tools. No matter the form these interactions take, the focus should remain on meeting the needs of others as customers for something we can offer. This idea should go beyond the thinking of current global connections such as ePals, sister schools, and so on., where our purpose is mainly to gain understanding of other cultures and individuals—the purpose here would be action oriented.

Overcoming Challenges

Students are often driven to help others. They want to do good work, or rather, work that promotes good things for others. Kids and young adults have in common the fact that they often dream of wanting to start their own business. They have heard of young entrepreneurs and are enticed by these exciting and praised global success stories. Wouldn't they all like to be the next Mark Zuckerberg, Steve Jobs, or better yet, Markus "Notch" Persson, the creator of Minecraft? How about Maddie Bradshaw, who owns M3 Girl Designs? In 2006, at the age of 10, Bradshaw started her own company that designs and sells Snap Caps, colorful bottle caps that can be worn as charms on necklaces, bracelets, and hairpins. In 2008, only a couple years after the inception of her company, her revenue was $1.6 million and she employed 25 people. Successful entrepreneurs know their market, they know who their potential customers are, and work to define how to meet their needs with a product or a service. Product-oriented learning is a natural fit for global opportunities and markets with a diverse group of potential customers.

We live in a world of possibilities with customers all around us. People need things—the world is changing, and there are constantly evolving opportunities to fill the gap with our creations or our knowledge. For educators, it is easy to see that we need to provide our students with the opportunities to meet the needs of others and to design possible products and services for others. Students need empathetic foresight—the ability to understand what is needed and wanted by others and the ability to ask the right questions to reach the desired end. As educators we want them to utilize their innate talents and develop the necessary skills to be able to do this on a global level—the level at which they will need to function in order to be successful. We are constantly examining what we do in classrooms with and for our students—how we teach, how we empower them to be in charge of their own learning and their future.

Outside the world of education, however, our parent community is sometimes not so sure that we need to change what we are doing. Parents want their children to be well educated and to be successful in the world that awaits them. They want their children to eventually move away from home with the ability of supporting themselves financially in an independent manner. Even with this as an expectation, the philosophy of parents concerning education is often that it is okay as is—if the way they learned was good enough for them, it will work just as well for their children.

If school leaders and teachers allow themselves to believe that if their parents are happy, there is no need to change, they are doing a disservice to their students. The challenge for all educators is to make this new way of learning come alive in a way that showcases the world of possibilities for our students. Take risks, ask questions, create prototypes, look for global markets—this is real-world learning that will make a difference in the lives of our students from a teacher perspective, and in the lives of our children from a parent's perspective.

Activity #1: Analyze Cause and Effect to Find Customers

Participants: Students, teachers, school administrative teams, district-level educators

Objective: It is helpful to understanding the cause-and-effect relationship pertinent to problems in order to create a marketable and viable solution and find a customer base. In this activity, participants will analyze a situation to find customers by looking first at the cause and the effect.

Materials

- Digital device to search and possibly create image of customer
- Chart paper and markers

Organization: Groups of two to four

Process (60 minutes): As a group, decide on a situation to use for this activity. (Search cause and effect headlines from news as an option.) Use the chart paper and sticky notes to brainstorm.

Analyze the Cause

- Who or what is the cause of this situation?
- Can we impact change with the cause? If so, how?

Analyze the Effect

- Who or what is being effected?
- Can we impact positive change with the effect?
- Is it possible to impact change with the affected? If so, how?

Is There a Causal Chain?

- Are there multiple cause and effect happenings that lead to a final result?

- If so, how can impacting one of the steps influence the outcome?
- Who is being effected along the chain?

And Our Customer Is . . .

- Create an image of a customer based upon the analysis using chart paper or computer.
- Share your customer with the larger group. Explaining the cause-and-effect process behind your decision on selecting the customer.

Reflection

- In what ways is this activity a viable approach to finding customers who need a product or service?
- What did you learn from this activity? Did anything about this activity surprise you?
- How could you use this activity in your academic setting?

ACTIVITY #2: A WORLD OF IDEAS AND SOLUTIONS— MAP OUT DIFFERENT NEEDS FOR THE SAME ISSUE

Participants: Students, teachers, school administrative teams, district-level educators

Objective: Global issues impact communities around the world in disparate ways. To be successful in product-oriented learning, students need to understand the needs and wants of the specific community, or communities, to which they are providing a service or marketing a product. This activity helps define the potential needs related to various geographic, economic, or cultural areas in solving a common problem.

Materials

- Digital tool with Internet access to conduct online searches
- Chart paper and markers

Organization: Partner activity

Process (50 minutes)

Choose a Global Issue

Determine a global issue or choose from one of the following: food crisis, water crisis, climate change, greater incidence of extreme weather, underemployment or unemployment, social and political instability, and so on.

Create a Chart

On chart paper create a table with the following columns.

Location	Specific Need	Possible Solution and Customer

"Google It" and Complete Chart

Do a quick search on your designated global issue specific to 5–10 various locations around the world. For instance: "Water crisis in Africa," "Water crisis in the United States," "Water crisis in Australia," and so on.

Chart, Compare, and Conclude

- How different are the needs of customers in different parts of the world?
- What are the ramifications in terms of potential customers?
- How can solving the problem in one location help bring understanding to another?
- What can be learned by each situation?
- How can the customer experience in one locale be of benefit to customers in another locale?

Reflection

- What did you learn from this activity? Did anything about this activity surprise you?
- How could you use this activity in your academic setting?

Activity #3: Visualize
Future Possibilities With Vowels

Participants: Students, teachers, school administrative teams, district-level educators

Objective: Leading the way in a fast-paced world of innovators and designers means looking to the future. What will people need and want as our world changes? As entrepreneurs, this vision is a critical piece of creating and maintaining products and services for an active client base. This activity is a way to brainstorm ideas with the future as the perspective for opportunity.

Materials

- Sticky notes (different colors if possible for each vowel)

Organization

- Divide participants into groups of three to four.
- Designate areas around room for postings of notes for each vowel (tables, walls, windows, etc.).

Process (45–60 minutes): There will be designated areas around the room to be used for each vowel. Groups will brainstorm ideas for each of the A-E-I-O-U categories and post their notes in the appropriate areas.

A—Analyze How the World Around Us Is Changing

Brainstorm some of the major ways the world is changing.

. . . consider natural changes on earth

. . . think about people, institutions, governments impacting change

. . . reflect on how changing global systems impact each other

E—Explore the Possibilities of New Customers

Who are the potential customers? For each possible customer analyze which type of entrepreneurial effort would meet the need. Social? Reciprocal?

I—Identify How These Changes and New Customers/Markets are Openings for New Opportunities

Change creates opportunity—think about new opportunities for each change listed above.

O—Orchestrate a Plan to Check the Feasibility of the Idea

What steps should you take to see if this is a valid idea?

Who is the authentic audience?

U—Utilize Your Connections and Resources

Who would you consider to be a mentor or an expert in this area?

Who would you consider to be a possible partner?

Is there a way to connect with potential customers?

What Does the Future Hold?

- How does looking ahead change our entrepreneurial perspective?
- Name entrepreneurs who have specifically benefitted from this look into the future.
- How does this approach lend a fresh approach to finding new customers and not replicating current business ideas?

Reflection

- What did you learn from this activity? Did anything about this activity surprise you?
- How could you use this activity in your academic setting?
- Would you revisit this activity to spark new ideas? How often?

Activity #4: I want to know what you know! Reciprocity in Learning

Participants: Students, teachers, school administrative teams, district level educators

Objective: Consider the value of students helping each other by sharing, teaching, and mentoring each other—as reciprocal customers. (Refer to the section in this chapter where sefoo.org is mentioned.) In this activity, participants will brainstorm ways to create these connections and opportunities for students on a global platform.

Materials

- Digital devices with Internet access
- Backchannel option: Today's Meet, Chatzy, Edmodo, Google+
  - In large groups, an option is to have a separate backchannel for each prompt.

Organization

- Conversation couples (change for every question if possible—left, right, forward, back, switch tables, move seats, etc.)
- Large group backchannel dialogue
- Large group facilitated reflection

Process (60 minutes): Participants will be prompted with a statement and related questions. After each prompt, 5 minutes will be given for "conversation couples" to spark and share ideas. Then 5 minutes will be designated for individual sharing on the backchannel.

Prompt 1: I Am Curious About the World!

- What would I like to learn from someone else around the world?

- What could this look like?
- How could I make it happen?

Prompt 2: I Have Something to Share!

- What do I have to offer others in different places around the world?
- What am I passionate about when considering positive change?
- How can I connect with others?

Prompt 3: Let's Create a Global Glimpse Together!

- What is a common global topic for which I would like to see a world perspective?
- How can a global perspective help me to understand current issues related to a subject/content area?
- What are ways I can spark this global discussion or presentation?

Prompt 4: I'll Teach You if You Teach Me!

- What is a situation you can think of where two parties are both student and teacher simultaneously?
- How could this be set up?

Possible Facilitator Created
Prompts Based on the Back-Channel Dialogue

- The facilitator may add prompts or questioning to dig deeper into what is trending in the group conversation.

Final Prompt: Sounds Great,
But I Need to Know More or Need Help!

- What are your questions about setting up?
- What would you need help with moving forward?

Reflection

As a group, discuss the following:

- What are the biggest takeaways from this activity?
- Did anything about this activity inspire you to implement any new ideas?
- How could you use this activity in your academic setting?
- How will you communicate what has resulted from trying this activity in your academic setting?
- How can we continue to share resources and document progress with these new ideas?

REFERENCES

Ritz, S. (2012, January 30). Green Bronx Machine: Growing our way into a new economy. Retrieved from https://www.youtube.com/watch?v=lcSL2yN39JM

Ritz, S. (2013, October 22). Harvesting hope. *Huffington Post.* http://www.huffingtonpost.com/stephen-ritz/green-bronx-machine_b_4124736.html

Schwartz, A. (2011, October 11). High school students build a farmer's market in a food desert. Fast Company & Inc. Retrieved from http://www.fastcoexist.com/1678622/high-school-students-build-a-farmers-market-in-a-food-desert

SEFOO. Retrieved June 11, 2015, from http://www.thresholdschool.org/our-approach.html

Stephen Ritz bio. (2015). *Huffington Post.* Retrieved June 11, 2015, from http://www.huffingtonpost.com/stephen-ritz/

United States Department of Agriculture (USDA). (2015). Food Deserts. Retrieved on June 11, 2015, from http://apps.ams.usda.gov/food deserts/fooddeserts.aspx

Van Meter, B. (2014, April 4). Filmmaker spotlight: Brendan Van Meter and Stephen Ritz of Green Bronx Machine. Real Food Media Contest. Retrieved from http://realfoodmedia.org/filmmaker-spotlight-brendan-van-meter-and-stephen-ritz-of-green-bronx-machine/

Welcome to Green Bronx Machine. (2011, May 31). Retrieved from https://www.youtube.com/watch?v=Cww_dUh5FUIO

Windsor Super Market. (2015). Retrieved June 11, 2015, from https://www.facebook.com/WindsorSuper/info?tab=overview

Zhao, Y. (2012). *World class learners: Educating creative and entrepreneurial students*. Thousand Oaks, CA: Corwin Press.

4

The Global Supply Chain

Others as Partners

by Homa Tavangar

"Coming together is a beginning, staying together is progress, and working together is success."

—Henry Ford

"Partners are for longer-term collaboration rather than a one-time transaction. Partners offer complementary skills and knowledge."

—Zhao (2012, p. 220)

Featured Case Study

Li & Fung Export Trading Company, Hong Kong, China

Li & Fung is Hong Kong's oldest Chinese-owned and largest export trading company. The company's core business has dramatically shifted every generation, in response to market needs. For example, in the 1980s, the competitive edge depended on controlling cost and quality for clients like Gap, Inc. and The Limited; 20 years later, the focus had shifted to "innovation, flexibility, and speed," manifested by their use of "borderless manufacturing" (Magretta, 1998). This means that parts and materials are sourced and processed in diverse locations, utilizing an effective global supply chain, or interconnected network of tasks and partner organizations each contributing a crucial, yet sometimes miniscule-seeming, link in a chain. Strengths are tapped, weaknesses are outsourced. No one location, expertise, or technology dominates the supply chain, or possesses every strength. So, when a jacket says, "Made in Indonesia," that more likely represents one step in a multilayered process of sourcing the best zippers from Japan, fabrics from Peru, yarns and threads from Vietnam, assemblers from Indonesia, designers from China and the United States, information systems in Estonia, and financial managers from Hong Kong, Singapore, and London. The "Made in" label today is as inadequate for capturing the jacket's actual production process as the four walls of a classroom are for offering effective global learning.

PRINCIPLES FOR GLOBAL SUPPLY CHAIN FOR WORLD CLASS LEARNING

- Collaborate
- Innovate
- Source
- Oversee
- Deliver
- Craft personalized products
- Tap the strengths of partnerships

That jacket comes to us through a process that involves multiple iterations of production, diverse expertise, far-flung locations, and curation of the best and varied technologies. Li & Fung sets the world standard for what an effective global supply chain should look and operate like. And their business model can teach some powerful lessons for setting up effective partnerships in a 21st century, creative, entrepreneurial, global education model.

The company's values statement reads:

> *We are a diverse global multinational with Asian roots and a proud entrepreneurial heritage. Our values guide our business every day. At our core, we are entrepreneurs with our customers' best interests at heart. We are humble, resourceful and innovative. Our people are at the center of our success and the source of our expertise. Building long-term relationships with our stakeholders is important to us. We care for the communities in which we live and work and they are an integral part of our extended family.* (Li & Fung, n.d.)

If you replace just a few words to suit your own heritage and educational environment, the statement could read:

> *We are a diverse global multinational* [learning community] *with Asian* [can be replaced with your local identity] *roots and a proud entrepreneurial heritage* [or whatever heritage you care to highlight: heritage of excellence, inquiry, close-knit community?]. *Our values guide our business* [teaching and learning] *every day. At our core, we are entrepreneurs* [teachers or learners; or just keep "entrepreneurs"] *with our customers'* [students'] *best interests at heart. We are humble, resourceful and innovative. Our people are at the center of our success and the source of our expertise. Building long-term relationships with our stakeholders is important to us. We care for the communities* [or, our community] *in which we live and work and they are an integral part of our extended family.*

Your class, school, or district might not adapt this values statement verbatim, but it illustrates that this global supply chain leader holds values quite similar to a thriving, entrepreneurial learning community. Perhaps even more telling for comparison to entrepreneurial learning and global partnerships is the company's "What We Do" principles:

- We collaborate.
- We innovate.
- We source.
- We oversee.
- We deliver.

Collaborate and Innovate

Looking at these principles in light of an entrepreneurial, global classroom, school, or district, certainly World Class Learners collaborate and innovate. In the case of Li & Fung, collaborating and innovating are essential to their long-term success as a global supply chain leader, placed at the front of their action list, not just an afterthought of a tradition-bound organization.

Source and Oversee

By "source," the third item on the "What We Do" list, they mean:

We source great products from suppliers around the world. We evaluate factories based on their capability to supply the right product and based on their commitment to quality, safety and compliance. We work with over 15,000 suppliers in multiple ways to meet our customers' needs.

In an education environment, the parallel idea could be to "curate," as in sourcing and choosing the best resources from a large pool of global innovation and always being on the lookout for better sources. The parallel to "oversee" for education comes from the vital role of teachers and other guides of the learning, discussed throughout this book and the series.

Deliver

The final step, "We Deliver," is described: *"We're not just about moving things from one place to another. We analyze each customer's needs, anticipate challenges, design options and set up contingency plans so they never have to worry about the journey."* Delivery, in this case, seems closely parallel to product-oriented learning: The goal in the final step is not a simple handing in of an assignment with few implications for wider learning, but creating a product for an authentic audience you care about.

Craft Personalized Products

Li and Fung's case represents a global supply chain model on a massive scale that's been continuously improved over decades, reaching millions of customers. At the other end of the spectrum lies another growing production trend—crafted-with-pride, small batch, creative, often personalized artisanal items such as those sold on the popular made-by-hand marketplace Etsy.com, or services for exchange such as those available via Taskrabbit.com or Airbnb.com. These might involve one person working out of their home who loves the product or service they sell or trade, reciprocating with another person they've never met, who also loves the product. The sales can be one-off, or they often create a community of enthusiasts whose crowd-sourced feedback on possible product improvements and pricing, as well lasting correspondence, social media mentions/endorsements, and reviews create a global supply chain reflecting the tastes of a new generation in a new form of commercial exchange. Indeed, some of these ventures fall under the Collaborative Consumption movement, where consumer values prioritize access, networking, sustainability, and relationships over ownership. In this model, "entire communities and cities around the world are using network technologies to do more with less by renting, lending, swapping, bartering, gifting and sharing products on a scale never before possible" (http://collaborativeconsumption.com/about).

Tap the Strengths of Partnerships

This spectrum from massive-scale to small-batch enterprise can light a way for a veritable education supply chain that can mirror—and question—the world's best practices as driven by market preferences. Among the key elements of their success is the ability to tap the strengths of partnerships for meaningful networking and exchange resulting in the best possible final product. As educators, we can consider how meaningful partnerships can help fuel the best possible learning, showing us that all the knowledge and skills don't need to come from within our own classrooms, but a collective sharing adds depth, beauty, higher standards, and new avenues for creativity to a complex process. This can involve tapping various networks, creating meaningful partnerships with organizations located across town or across the planet, breaking down cognitive processes into specialization areas, and communications made more effective through diverse channels to launch a process of "borderless learning."

PRINCIPLES FOR ESTABLISHING AN EFFECTIVE EDUCATIONAL PARTNERSHIP

- Reflect on the principles of clarity, reciprocity, and engagement
- Prioritize solidarity over charity
- Make at least a 1-year commitment
- Set goals and integrate them
- Connect classroom to classroom, not just pupil to pupil
- Consider common learning and action themes
- Measure success by how well the class does when handling tech glitches

Just as some of the most respected business publications have studied best practices of developing a global supply chain; likewise, effective educational partnerships are beginning to be studied and identified by coalitions that want to see these efforts work. The National Network of Schools in Partnership has developed the following useful framework that shows the crucial overlap of strategic engagement, reciprocity, and clarity of purpose to the strength of a relationship. As partnerships—near or far—are pursued, determine their value or strength by the intersection of these three simple guideposts.

The excellent questions for reflection under each of the principles, which fall under the headings Clarity, Reciprocity, and Engagement, offer an ideal starting point for your team to fill out as you begin an effective educational partnership. Here are a few more issues to consider before setting up an educational partnership:

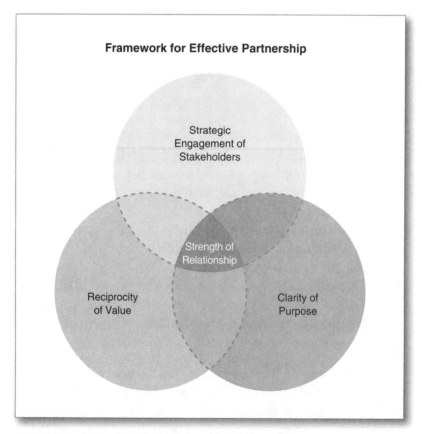

Framework for Effective Partnership

Strategic Engagement of Stakeholders

Strength of Relationship

Reciprocity of Value

Clarity of Purpose

SOURCE: National Network of Schools in Partnership (2014).

- Prioritize solidarity over charity. When engaging in school-to-school partnerships, consider those in the partnership as your peers, where mutual learning will take place. A desire for charity may naturally emerge from interaction, but if you begin with the position that you will "help" the other children, your students will assume a superior, benefactor role, which is not conducive to collaboration and learning from each other.
- Make at least a 1-year commitment. By making a longer-term commitment, you will set out to get to know your partners and deepen the learning and relationship beyond a one-off fascination of those who seem so different.
- Set goals and integrate them. Identify a few tangible outcomes (academic as well as social) you hope to realize from the partnership, and where you can integrate the partnership and collaboration into the general curriculum. For example, if students create a video in the foreign language they are learning, students in the partner class can evaluate it, and conversation also can be practiced in videocalls; lab reports for science classes can integrate observations of global partners experiencing a different climate; product assessment, out-loud reading, or book discussion can take place with the partner class.
- Connect classroom to classroom, not just pupil to pupil. Even if you are engaging in individual projects or pen-pals, make this a united, group effort. You'll begin to see variations across people in their classroom, work through any individual disappointments, better sustain the partnership, and be able to encourage individual efforts from among your students.
- Consider common learning and action themes. For example, you could have a joint project related to peace, the environment, or creating more inclusive classrooms (antibullying), concerns that children on both sides of the partnership will share. This can serve as a proactive platform for working together, and it helps get to know each other on a deeper level.

- Partnership shouldn't depend on the technology; in fact, success might be measured by how well the class does when handling glitches. Be ready to plan around asynchronous time zones, lack of adequate bandwidth and Internet connection, sound and video limitations, long delays in receiving replies to letters or e-mails, and general miscommunication. Discuss these possibilities; look for backup solutions (Tavangar & Morales, 2014).

WHAT CAN AN EDUCATIONAL PARTNERSHIP FOR GLOBAL LEARNING LOOK LIKE?

This chapter's opening story traced the production process of a jacket you might purchase at a store like The Gap. As products get more complex, the global supply chain grows with it. For example Boeing describes the production process of its 787 Dreamliner, its more fuel-efficient jet:

> More than 50 of the world's most capable top-tier supplier partners work with Boeing to bring innovation and expertise to the 787 program. They all have been involved since the early detailed design phase of the program and are connected virtually at 135 sites around the world. (Boeing, n.d.)

Even an industry behemoth like Boeing acknowledges that effective partnerships among many suppliers are crucial to the best possible final outcome. Almost no industry or innovation can afford to have its people or components operate in isolation. Likewise, engaging in K–12 education partnerships isn't just a more interesting way of learning; it's a crucial part of building the skills needed to contribute to the new economy, whether as an entrepreneur or a corporate employee.

Like the various supply chain models seeking to create the optimal product quality and price, educational partnerships can take on many forms, varying by levels of intensity and engagement, and these depend on a number of factors, including willingness of leadership and teaching staff on both sides to engage in partnerships, perceived benefits to students, how parallel the partnering schools may be to each other as far as socioeconomic conditions, academic demands, and technological capacity.

Here are some examples of partnership strategies in the context of World Class Learning according to setting: For classroom teachers, school leaders, and system leaders; as well as consideration of different realities—thinking (beginning), implementing (intermediate), and expanding (advanced) are outlined in the next section.

STRATEGIES FOR ESTABLISHING AN EFFECTIVE EDUCATIONAL PARTNERSHIP

In the Classroom

Skype in the Classroom and Mystery Skype (Thinking About Partnerships—Beginning)

If you've never tried a global class-to-class partnership, consider starting with Skype in the Classroom. This popular platform contains thousands of lesson plans and ideas so that the conversations with other classrooms can be integrated into broader learning. Skype in the Classroom showcase features some of the best lesson plans for global education (http://education.skype.com/collections). Teachers or entrepreneurial students also can create their own project that suits specific circumstances and interests. Second-graders in Atlanta might share their show-and-tell with a classroom in Accra. Middle schoolers in Mexico City can construct antibullying and other social-emotional learning strategies with their peers in New Delhi. Classes reading Lois Lowry's *Number the Stars* (or fiction set anywhere that isn't their hometown) might Skype with students in Denmark for an ongoing book discussion to get a sense of the place they are reading about. And if time zones pose a problem for real-time learning, stay within your hemisphere, record your conversation prompts and results, or seek other creative ways to connect. MysterySkype offers a simple guessing game for communicating with another class: "The aim of the game is to guess the location of the other classroom by asking each other questions" (MysterySkype, n.d.). Once you've played with the other class, you might decide to take on more meaningful projects together, and launch a longer partnership.

Pen Pals (Thinking About Partnerships—Beginning)

Whether through exchanging e-mails or handwritten letters, pen pal correspondence with individuals or classes around the world can serve as a beginning step in building a global partnership, since it starts with the building block of personal communication; but this can grow to more impactful exchanges to benefit learning. Writing to pen pals can improve reading and writing, while offering opportunities for making lifelong friends and dispelling myths about places and cultures we may never have had personal contact with. Your own (or colleagues') network of friends and family with ties to schools around the world might serve as the best starting point for locating pen pals. Or, reputable organizations like ePals, World Wise Schools, a program of the U.S. Peace Corps, People to People International, School-to-School International, and Students of the World can help facilitate partnerships via pen pals.

Classrooms on Twitter (Thinking About Partnerships—Beginning or Intermediate)

Just as the world's most admired entrepreneurs interact on Twitter, so do entrepreneurial classrooms. The 140-character limit has not inhibited meaningful interaction, even among the youngest students. For example, kindergartners in Heidi Echternacht's class in New Jersey have "play partners" in Cairo, Egypt, with whom they communicate through Twitter and occasionally via Skype. Starting with simple conversation prompts like "What do you play at recess?" or "What do you see out the window?" kids living in such different cultures and environments become demystified and relationships might grow from there. Other #kinderchat prompts include the #LookingClosely hashtag and project, inspired by Frank Serafini's *Looking Closely* book series. Collaboration and communication via Twitter helps students take a closer look at their natural surroundings, ask questions, and use their imaginations. These can serve as stepping stones to becoming alert to possibilities and needs—the foundation of entrepreneurial learning. For more, see The Looking Closely collaboration site. For high school students, Twitter serves as an ideal way to connect with current events and activists they might be studying (as in the DeforestACTION project highlighted later in this chapter), to begin a dialogue and personalize issues that otherwise would feel far-away, and model a productive use of social media.

Global Read-Aloud (Implementing Partnerships—Intermediate)

The Global Read Aloud (GRA; n.d.) is a worldwide book club that started in 2010 and as of 2014 had grown to more than 4,100 facilitators in 30+ different countries, translating into roughly 244,000 students, representing 100,000 more participants than the previous year (http://www.globalreadaloud.com/2014/09/the-1-month-countdown-has-begun-for.html). Students from kindergarten through college level read a pre-determined book during a set 4-week period, while making as many global connections as possible. Teachers can choose any communications platform for their class collaboration, such as Twitter, Skype, Edmodo, the Global Read Aloud wikispaces page, e-mail, regular mail, or Kidblog to connect with one, two, or more classrooms from around the world. Dynamic conversations on books, creative products for sharing the love of the literature, and discovering new ideas across boundaries represent just a few of the ingredients that contribute to GRA's popularity.

Joint Science Project With Various Schools Around the World (Implementing Partnerships—Intermediate)

The Center for Innovation in Engineering and Science Education (CIESE) at Stevens Institute of Technology in Hoboken, New Jersey, in partnership with the Edison Venture Fund and NJ Technology and Engineering Educators Association set up a "telecollaborative project" to introduce students in Grades 9–12 to systems engineering. Stevens Institute provided the curricular content for background knowledge; then students were to create reassembly instructions and diagrams that partner classrooms worldwide used in attempting to reconstruct the device. We consider the reconstructing activity to be on the "intermediate" level of partnership, and in the cases where materials provided by the project would be used by teachers and students to create more advanced collaborative designs, this would be more advanced, demonstrating how global supply chain in an education setting can work.

DeforestACTION, Mapping the Mangroves and Online Model U.N. (Classroom, School or District, Beginner, Intermediate, or Expanding—Advanced)

DeforestACTION, a project of TakingITGLobal (tigweb.org, which hosts numerous collaborative, global learning programs), serves as an educational and action platform for meaningful, global, collaborative problem solving by exploring issues of deforestation in Borneo, engaging thousands of students from around the world in this very real environmental crisis. We found the suite of possibilities through this program could serve an individual classroom, or could be embraced by entire schools or districts, whether just starting out with global partnerships or ready to go deeper with an integrated partnership.

The program contains teacher resources, examples of student projects, and the DeforestACTION Virtual Classroom with K–12 lesson plans and learning activities for those just starting to think about global partnerships, or wanting to add-on to current curriculum to more advanced commitment.

As part of the program, Earthwatchers marries exciting technology with unfolding science and environmental activism. Here students can monitor the rainforests of Borneo through satellite imagery, mark changes in land patterns over a period of time, and report disturbances via a collaborative website and social media. Collaboration and partnership aren't add-ons in this program, but integral to "Earth watching," to taking real, not simulated responsibility for saving sections of the rainforest. The Earthwatchers Promo Video of students from Cleveland District State High School in Australia (2012) who have been so impacted by their participation in the program conveys the entrepreneurial learning and profound impact this project has had, guided by the wisdom and commitment of a terrific teacher.

Other elements of the program include the DeforestACTION Collaboration Centre, a space for students and youth to dialogue, blog, share photos, connect with the "Eco Warriors" and collaborate with peers from around the world; online events in real time, and additional action tools for students to extend their learning through further involvement.

Mapping the Mangroves, a project of the Qatar Foundation International in partnership with Conservation International, like DeforestACTION, focuses on raising awareness, conversation, and action around environmental preservation of threatened ecosystems using GPS tracking technology so that student learning and outcomes revolve around vital, real global needs.

Online Model United Nations (O-MUN): While Model U.N. conferences can be cost-prohibitive or pose other logistical challenges for many students to attend in person, O-MUN is committed to democratizing this popular academic program, "keeping the focus squarely on mentorship, discussion, collaboration and high academic standards" (Online Model United Nations website welcome page, n.d.). Students come together virtually to debate and collaborate around the world's most pressing issues in an open, social, participatory environment. An O-MUN video conveys the infectious enthusiasm for this collaboration that isn't bound by location or resources (O-MUN, 2013).

In the School

School-to-School Partnerships Among
Disparate Schools (Beginner, Intermediate or Advanced)

When the Packer Collegiate Institute, a top, independent K–12 school in Brooklyn, New York, embarked on a school partnership with the Ndonyo-Wasin Primary School in the Samburu region of Kenya, a part of the world that is about as different from Brooklyn as can be imagined, school leaders knew the venture would take patience, imagination, and long-term commitment. Ndonyo-Wasin has limited access to electricity and no Internet, so real-time communication between students is impossible, and the typical school connection platforms aren't an option, either. Instead, students from both schools write letters, paint portraits made from photographs, and make videos to exchange with each other. Students in New York learn a few words of Samburu, the local language, Swahili, one of the national languages, and about the geography of the Samburu region of Kenya. By learning about everyday life of the Samburu, they are able to reflect on their own life circumstances, as well as on disparities of life within New York City. So, while learning about such a remote area that even most Kenyans will not visit, the Packer students build their appreciation of the diversity of life in their own city and in the wider world. A small nonprofit, The Thorn Tree Project, dedicated to this remote region of East Africa, also supports the partnership.

Teachers and administrators reached a consensus that building a relationship and learning about Kenya would be systematically integrated into the scope and sequence of the lower (elementary) school. With teacher input, Packer undertook a redesign of the curriculum. For example, the kindergarteners learn about family structures in this community: that they are nomadic, and that their parents are herders, and so the children board at school. The third graders study the native tribes of the local, New York City area, and make comparisons between the Lenape American Indians and the Samburu tribe, their reliance on the land and livestock, and why one culture dies out and other doesn't. Results from both schools are self-published into books that the schools share with each other. Teachers at Packer are careful not to exoticize this society where warrior-age men still dress in traditional clothing with beads and bright colors, and maintain rituals and cultural customs that are essential in their culture. By keeping the learning grounded in empathy, humility, and appreciation, the children can understand more profoundly the challenges and joys of a starkly contrasting way of life.

School-to-School Partnerships Among
Schools With Common Courses of Study (Intermediate)

Connect All Schools, an initiative spurred by the historic speech by President Obama in Cairo, Egypt, in June 2009 to encourage all schools to engage in global partnerships by 2016, highlights examples of global connections at various stages of sophistication throughout its website. These can be simple, such as two high school economics classes from two sister cities sharing and discussing economic realities in their local environments to deepen knowledge of what economic decisions can look like in practice. Despite the relative simplicity of working on economics homework or discussing chapters in a textbook between Seattle, Washington, and Christchurch, New Zealand, the exchange adds value by shedding light on concepts like central banking, money supply, and inflation based on diverse decisions government leaders and the public make.

Partnerships can grow in complexity with specific projects and assignments, such as those facilitated by Challenge 20/20, which pairs two or more schools of any type of background (public or private, one from the United States and others outside the United States) to work on projects that help find local solutions to one of 20 global problems. Challenges are set up so they are age-appropriate for K–12 participation and work best when classrooms feel that they are doing real work that contributes to global solutions.

Before-, During-, or After-School Vegetable Garden
Cultivation—Global Partners, Local Customers (Beginning,
Intermediate, or Advanced—Depending on Level of Participation)

The ANIA Children's Land Project/Tierra de Niños, facilitated by global partnership leader iEARN (www.us.iearn.org),
brings together participants from over 20 countries, ranging
from Australia to Yemen, for collaborative learning with facilitators in Peru and the United States to share home or school
gardening experiences, and learn from the agricultural wisdom
of indigenous people of Peru for developing local, sustainable gardening practices. Launched by Peruvian organization,
Tierra de Niños (TiNi), partners plant a TiNi ("teeny"), which
is a plot of land divided into three parts to benefit the environment ("la naturaleza"), the community ("la comunidad"),
and one self ("mi mismo").

The TiNi is exciting as a product-oriented partnership
model. While cultivating a garden, participants in the iEARN
program share best practices, encouragement, and build a
virtual community around their shared activity. They apply
learning in science, Spanish, language arts, and/or social
studies to a very real product. In the Jardin por Jardin video
(2011) made by 12-year-olds in Seattle, we see the creation of
a video in Spanish itself, as well as the garden, serve as reflection of product-oriented learning in the context of a global
partnership.

In the School System

Exchange Programs Sponsored by
National Governments (Beginning, Intermediate
or Advanced—Depending on Level of Participation)

Teacher and student exchange programs facilitated by
national governments, like those in Denmark, Australia,
and the British Council's Connecting Classrooms program
that links schools in the United Kingdom to other schools
in over 40 countries, might serve as an excellent partnership
resource for a school system or district. Participation can

offer professional development, teacher exchange across countries, programs for students, curricular material that spurs connection across borders, and schoolwide resources that can shift the whole school or district's culture. The U.S. State Department offers more narrowly focused programs specifically for teachers or individual students, as non-profit organizations facilitate most of the school and student exchanges in districts across the United States. Check with the the Council on Standards for International Educational Travel to help U.S. high school students to study abroad or to find reputable organizations that facilitate students from abroad to study in the U.S. high schools can make the welcoming and hosting of exchange students from various countries one of the milestones of a broader global learning and partnership plan.

School-to-School, District-to-District, or Sister-City
Exchange Programs (Beginning, Intermediate, or
Advanced—Depending on Level of Participation)

The Marlborough School of Los Angeles and Beijing No. 4 High School, both prestigious schools in their respective cities, engage in student-to-student exchange where students from each school attended classes at the "sister school," and students reside with host families during their stay, in addition to their partnerships with other schools in geographically and demographically diverse cities. For example, Marlborough has run immersive exchanges with a school in Paris and another with Northlands School in Buenos Aires, and Beijing No. 4 has a long-standing exchange with the University of Chicago Lab School. The exchanges make up one prong in a larger, strategic global education initiative of the schools, where administration and teachers at both schools have made adaptive, long-term revisions to curriculum, including added depth of global issues and diversity of literature, as well as reflecting on further means to integrate culturally relevant topics.

As Marlborough Dean of Student Life and Spanish instructor, Regina Rosi explained,

Our goal is to streamline exchange programs and foreign travel. With the exchanges, teachers and students bring back new awareness and depth to global and language studies, so it's a more effective educational experience and significantly less costly, as students participate in homestays, and cultural experiences occur in the context of student life at the high school and being part of a local community; instead of paying for the prearranged activities of a tour operator. (Rosi, 2014)

Students from Marlborough who participated in the most recent trips lead discussions and meetings for peers and faculty with the intention of inspiring further collaborations. A visual arts teacher is building a visual art exchange to involve Marlborough students posting their art online and Beijing No. 4 students using that art as an essay writing prompt; and vice-versa, with Marlborough students interpreting art posted by Beijing No. 4 students.

GLOBAL NOMADS GROUP

Global Nomads Group (GNG) is an international nonprofit organization that engages and empowers young people worldwide through interactive videoconferencing, webcasting, social networking, gaming, and participatory filmmaking. The use of multimedia serves as a vehicle for global awareness and peace making. GNG's semester and year-long virtual exchange programs between students in North America and their peers in Sub-Saharan Africa, Central and South East Asia, the Middle East and North Africa (MENA) encompass work on rebuilding efforts in Haiti, science collaborations in the Gulf nations, and a participatory arts project to cover the National Mall in Washington, DC, with 1,000,000 handmade bones to raise awareness of the ongoing humanitarian crisis in the Democratic Republic of the Congo. Participants in these social impact partnerships are also brought together in virtual town hall meetings via videoconference to discuss and debate international issues.

Overcoming Challenges

As we considered the biggest challenges in establishing successful school partnerships, the term *asynchronicities* wove through them, as a common theme. Awareness at the outset that you will be overcoming so many asynchronous conditions can help you to (1) know you're not alone, and (2) know that you can overcome barriers since so many others have before you. Often, just knowing these two facts can help one overcome big perceived obstacles. Here are some of the challenges you might encounter:

Challenges of Time

- You are likely in different time zones, so one group of students might be starting out the day, and the partner school is at a different part of theirs, so they may be tired, or have other demands.
- If you are on opposite seasons, your discussions of a budding spring or hot summer may not be relatable— but you can turn this into an exploration with the partner class.
- The other class might have a very different way their school day is organized, such as in long blocks, whereas your day may require switching from subject to subject every 45 minutes.

Challenges of Culture

- Can you tolerate partnering with a single-sex school, or one that has clearly delineated roles for boys versus girls, or requires girls to wear certain coverings that boys don't wear? Would your girls cover their arms or head out of respect during a videoconference or is this out of the question?
- Do the holiday periods in the partner school get in the way of your desired period of interaction?

- Communication styles in the culture of the partner school may call for avoiding eye contact or might regard enthusiastic hand-raising or waving as ill-mannered. To you this may seem to slow down the flow of conversation over a short 20-minute video chat. To smooth any misperceptions, try to familiarize yourself with some of the communication styles of that culture beforehand, especially by trying to poll adults with knowledge of the culture, either through personal interactions or even through blogs, reaching out via Twitter, or cultural communication experts at local business schools. Erin Meyer (2014) shares communication lessons she learned as an American living in Paris instructing Japanese students in her *New York Times* article, "Looking Another Culture in the Eye."

Challenges of Language

- Do you need to speak the same language fluently to accomplish your partnership goals?
- Are accents or speaking styles clear to each other?
- Or, would you prefer to not speak the same language fluently and practice foreign language skills with the partner class?

Challenges of Technology

- Is it crucial that the partner school or class has a reliable source of electricity and Internet?
- Does the Internet connection need to be high-speed, broadband in order to support clear video chatting, cloud-based collaborative work, the newest software applications, and real-time sharing?
- When you send an e-mail or other form of communication, how quickly do you expect the reply? Be aware that e-mail culture can vary widely from country to country, and this can take some adjusting on both sides.

/B!

Challenges of Curriculum and Learning Culture

- Are you looking for a partner that shares a similar curriculum, such as IB, AP, or Montessori?
- Are you looking for a partner that shares a similar level of academic rigor and academic expectations?
- Do you want to work with a partner that has joined similar networks (like Challenge 20/20, iEARN, or Taking-ITGlobal) or whose teachers have received some of the same training as teachers at your school?

Knowing that these asynchronicities are possible can test your resolve, but they also can prepare you realistically for challenges. As you know yourself, your class and your school or district culture, you will begin to realize which of these factors you can tolerate, and which might pose too great a barrier for a successful partnership. For example, consider if communicating with students in certain time zones will be too disruptive for the flow of your class. This can help pinpoint a location from which to seek a partner class. Do you prefer to meet students who have a similar view as far as gender roles, or would you like to open your students' eyes and show them how differently other cultures see the roles of boys and girls and have them grapple with those worldviews? Would you like to work through an intermediary organization to facilitate the partnership or be independent of an outside agency?

REFLECTION

The world's most successful businesses have figured out that partnering with diverse companies to build their global supply chain helps maximize results to construct the best possible product, whether it's a jacket or an airplane. Imagine what results would occur if we took the best know-how in the world, collaborated with diverse learners, and partnered to solve problems together: This might result in fostering the best learners. Why not learn from these best-practices to create successful educational partnerships?

While supply chain leaders like Li & Fung and Boeing look to minimize cost and maximize efficiency and productivity, benchmarks for successful school partnerships, determined by the strength of relationships, are found at the intersection of clarity of purpose, reciprocity of value, and engagement of key stakeholders. In other words, as each example in this chapter showed us, whatever the role of technology or demographic profile of participants, partnerships ultimately rested on the human relationships that came from working together; how fruitful interaction was perceived to be, and what meaning the participants got from their engagement with each other. More than ever, with the shifting needs of a connected, global economy, these factors are no longer "nice-to-have," but become essential, or "need-to-have" skills and experiences. How does partnership help advance your vision of a global learning experience?

ACTIVITY #1: PLANNING CONSIDERATIONS FOR A STRONG PARTNERSHIP

Participants: Teachers, school administrative teams, or district-level educators

Objective: Chapter 5 shares a "Framework for Effective Partnership" that can help serve as a planning tool for any school that is considering beginning a partnership with another school, or already has one in place, and would like to strengthen it. This exercise offers a chance for filling in and envisioning the Framework to advance your particular circumstances. When you have achieved some clarity around purpose, reciprocity, and how you will engage with stakeholders, then a global partnership makes sense: It can help advance academic objectives and not feel like one more add-on that is isolated from the core of learning. This activity offers the time and space for filling in a framework that makes sense for your school or district.

Materials

- Colored markers
- Flipcharts for each group

Organization: Groups of four to six

Process (60 minutes total—or this could extend into a half-day staff retreat)

Have each group answer the questions that accompany the Framework for Effective Partnership. When answering these questions that fall under three general categories, try to answer them based on your *actual* circumstances, as well as your *ideal* scenario (minimum 30 minutes):

A. Clarity of Purpose

How does your school's mission inspire the work of partnership?

How do you articulate why your school engages in partnership?

How do you assess the impact of your partnerships?

B. Strategic Engagement of Stakeholders

How does your strategic vision encompass partnership and community engagement?

How many stakeholders are involved in the success of your partnerships—students, faculty, administrators, alumni, parents, trustees, school board members, wider community members like businesses and civic organizations?

How does the work of partnership enrich learning?

✓ C. **Reciprocity of Value**

What is the value for each partner in the partnership?

Where does the partnership occur—in single or multiple locations?

Is the partnership framed around collaboration, rather than helping?

Reflection and Next Steps (minimum 30 minutes): Share the results of your small-group discussion with the other groups. How much divergence and how much overlap do you find in the responses? Are you ready to integrate the best or consensus responses into one coherent Framework for your school or district? Once the groups come together to share, are the divergences rooted in fundamental differences of vision or are they easy to overcome? Reflect on the process you've just undertaken and how this can benefit your school and your students.

This exercise can be repeated with high school students, in order to assess their stake in meaningful partnerships and compare outlooks on the value of the partnerships.

ACTIVITY #2: REACH OUT TO POTENTIAL PARTNERS/ GROW YOUR PLN VIA TWITTER (45–60 MINUTES)

Participants: Teachers, school administrative teams, or district-level educators

Objective: Twitter can serve as a powerful and substantive tool for building partnerships for your school as well as for your own professional learning, in spite of its 140-character limit per tweet. The experience of using social media toward productive and positive outcomes also can serve as a model for your students, who by age 13 almost inevitably are active on one social media platform or another. The objective of this activity is to open a personal Twitter account and begin to follow admired colleagues, join a Professional Learning Network (PLN), and find other schools or classes preferably in another country that might share learning goals with yours. If you already are active on Twitter, this is a chance to deepen and widen your networks and engagements.

Materials

- Smartphone, tablet, or computer that are Internet enabled to start tweeting.

Organization

Orientation of basic Twitter guidelines as a group; then work individually—opening a Twitter account, exploring various accounts on Twitter, engaging with others. Then come together and share experiences.

Process

Ten-Minute Twitter Tutorial (10 minutes): Get to know how to contact someone; use hashtags; look for topics of interest. For those who are brand-new, take a few minutes to open an account.

Twitter Exploration (approx. 20 minutes):

Get a little lost in the world of Twitter.

Try to determine an objective (e.g., Do you want to connect with other English teachers? The design-thinking community? Makers? Kindergarten teachers/classes? STEM enthusiasts? Or would you like to enrich your study of the Arab Spring? Understand diverse perspectives on the marijuana legalization debate? Or explore how to get involved in a social issue you care about, or help after a recent natural disaster?)

Once you've determined a topic or two of interest, begin following key accounts.

Engage (i.e., send a tweet, ask a question, respond to something recently tweeted) with people you admire or care to debate with.

What have you learned during this short time?

Reflection (approx. 15 minutes): Share what you learned with the larger group. Were you able to find a PLN to connect to? Will you be joining a Twitterchat around a particular topic or group? Does this seem like a worthwhile way for you to begin engaging with new partners? Would you share some of this learning with your (high school and up) students to model meaningful social media interaction? Set a specific time, like 30 minutes per week if possible, to dedicate to building your network and learning via Twitter.

Next Steps: Determine one area of activity which you will decide to pursue, either for developing a classroom or school partnership, or for your own professional development. Be ready to share this with the larger group. By sharing with the group, there's a much greater chance the activity will "stick," for longer-term benefit.

References

Boeing. (n.d.). Boeing 787 dreamliner provides new solutions for airlines, passengers. Retrieved from http://www.boeing.com/boeing/commercial/787family/background.page

Collaborative Consumption. (n.d.). Retrieved from http://www.collaborativeconsumption.com/about/

Earthwatchers Promo. (2012, July). Retrieved from https://www.youtube.com/watch?v=Nj1r383vVRk

Global Read Aloud. (n.d.). Retrieved from http://www.globalreadaloud.com/2014/09/the-1-month-countdown-has-begun-for.html.

Jardin por Jardin [Video]. (2011, July 26). Retrieved from https://www.youtube.com/watch?v=6-0lWr5I2sI&feature=youtu.be

Li & Fung. (n.d.). Our values. Retrieved from http://www.lifung .com/about-us/lf-at-a-glance

Magretta, J. (1998, September). Fast, global, and entrepreneurial: Supply chain management, Hong Kong style. *Harvard Business Review.* Retrieved from http://hbr.org/1998/09/fast-global-and-entrepre neurial-supply-chain-management-hong-kong-style/ar/1

Meyer, E. (2014, September 14). Looking another culture in the eye. *New York Times,* p. BU8. Retrieved from http://www.nytimes .com/2014/09/14/jobs/looking-another-culture-in-the-eye .html?module=Search&mabReward=relbias%3Ar%2C%7B%22 1%22%3A%22RI%3A8%22%7D

Mystery Skype. (n.d.). Retrieved from https://education.skype.com/ mysteryskype

National Network of Schools in Partnership. (2014). NNSP Partnership Framework. Retrieved from http://schoolsinpartnership.org/ framework

O-MUN. 2013, May 21. https://www.youtube.com/watch?v=v INlL5GaO48#t=73

Online Model United Nations Welcome Page. (n.d.). http://online modelunitednations.org/

Rosi, R. Personal communication. (2014, October 6).

Tavangar, H., & Morales, B. (2014). *The global education toolkit for elementary learners.* Thousand Oaks, CA: Corwin.

Zhao, Y. (2012). *World class learners: Educating creative and entrepreneurial students.* Thousand Oaks, CA: Corwin Press.

RESOURCES

ANIA Children's Land Project/Tierra de Niños, https://collaborate .iearn.org/space-2/group-87/about

Beijing No. 4 High School, http://www.bhsf.cn/index.php?id=103

British Council, Connecting Classrooms Programme, https:// schoolsonline.britishcouncil.org/programmes-and-funding/ linking-programmes-worldwide/connecting-classrooms

Center for Innovation in Engineering and Science Education (CIESE), http://www.ciese.org/

Challenge 20/20, http://www.nais.org/Articles/Pages/Challenge- 20-20.aspx

Connect All Schools, connectallschools.org

Council on Standards for International Educational Travel, http://www.csiet.org

DeforestACTION, http://dfa.tigweb.org/

ePals, http://www.epals.com

✓ Global Nomads Group, http://gng.org/

Global Read Aloud, http://www.globalreadaloud.com/

Global Read Aloud wikispaces page, http://globalreadaloud.wiki spaces.com/

Global School Partners, http://www.globalschoolpartners.org.au/what-we-do/

iEARN , http://www.iearn.org/

Kidblog, http://kidblog.org/home/

Kinder Chats, http://www.kinderchat.org/#!PROJECT-POND/c1z4y

Looking Closely Collaboration website, http://kidblog.org/Looking Closely/

Mapping the Mangroves, mappingthemangroves.org

✓ Marlborough School, http://www.marlborough.org/

✓ Meyer, E. (2014). The culture map: Breaking through the invisible boundaries of global business. New York, NY: Public Affairs.

Mystery Skype, #MysterySkype, https://education.skype.com/mysteryskype

✓ Online Model United Nations, http://onlinemodelunitednations.org/

People to People International, http://www.ptpi.org

School-to-School International, sts-international.org

Skype in the Classroom, https://education.skype.com/

Skype in the Classroom showcase, https://education.skype.com/collections

Students of the World, http://www.studentsoftheworld.info/menu_schools.php3

TakingITGlobal, https://www.tigweb.org/

Thorn Tree Project, http://www.thorntreeproject.org/

✓ U.S. State Department Exchange Programs, http://exchanges.state.gov/us/exchange-experience

✓ World Wise Schools, http://www.peacecorps.gov/wws/about/

5

Building Sustainable Global Connections

by Gabriel F. Rshaid

Featured Case Study

World Class Learners
Writing Team, Thousand Oaks, CA

By now readers know that every chapter of this series begins with a story illustrating some aspect of implementation of the chapter's theme. In this case, the story is about adults. The writing team responsible for this book is made up of five coauthors, and our editor. With the exception of two of the members of the team who had seen each other in person

(Continued)

(Continued)

once, we had never met before getting together face-to-face for a writing retreat to start developing this project. One of us lives in a foreign country, and four of us were born outside the United States. Despite the difference in backgrounds and geographical locations, there are numerous people connections among ourselves, and from our first conversations, we found a surprisingly high number of people that many of us knew or had worked with, personally or through the Internet. When we started the formal work of pooling our ideas together and starting to lay out the groundwork for the development of this three-book series, we immediately had a strong sense of rapport and seldom, if at all, had any discrepancies regarding principles and educational ideas. All of this despite the fact that our backgrounds are very diverse, that the educational systems in which we work are very different and that, age wise, we are not members of the "digital generation," and therefore, we can be considered what Mark Prensky calls "digital immigrants." We can safely say that we are living examples of a globally connected group that shares significant values and beliefs.

In attempting to deconstruct what made possible such an immediately strong connection amongst our team members who had mostly not worked with each other and who were able to hit the ground running in terms of the development of the project, it can be concluded that it was not just by chance that we were able to gel easily together as a team. The reason for this is that every one of us, in our own way, truly view the global world as being full of opportunities and have intentionally taken advantage of every chance that we have had to stretch our horizons and try to enjoy the interconnected world. All of us have sought opportunities to travel personally and professionally, we are all avid readers, we enjoy learning about other cultures, we have visited schools in different parts of the world, all of us speak at least one foreign language and dabble at some others, and in general, embrace globalization for what it is, an unlimited learning playing field.

We also reflected that we are outliers. Our schooling did not prepare us or predispose us favorably for our global mindset. Each one of us is almost an accident, a byproduct of circumstances and inner desires that took us on our journey not because of, but despite of, our school formation. The whole objective of this series of books is that world class learners are no longer accidents, but intentional outcomes of the schooling process.

Principles for Building Sustainable Global Connections

- Increase cultural awareness
- Understand the complexity and possibilities of a global world
- Be agile
- Move toward a worldview of opportunities

As we have extensively covered throughout the book, the global dimensions of education are acquiring increasing importance, hand-in-hand with a world that has effectively obliterated frontiers, shortened distances with dazzling speed amidst a breathtaking pace of change. It is only natural that educators have been called out to embrace globalization as a new mantra, and as such, we have all been witnesses to innumerable well-intentioned efforts to set up exchange programs, Skype connections, global collaborative projects, and a seemingly almost infinite flavor of attempts to effectively involve our students in a way that makes them fully fledged global citizens of the 21st century.

Many of the phrases included in the previous paragraph were intentionally playing on the clichés that are a byproduct of the proliferation of such initiatives, once again, a logical consequence of the drive to rush to establish globalization programs at every age level within the school system. In the process, and almost inevitably, as was the case with the introduction of technology for learning, much of the focus was on the initiatives themselves and not on the underlying educational objectives that were pursued through the introduction of those projects and ideas.

Looking back upon our group of writers and what made us actively pursue global connections ourselves in our work, traveling, attending conferences, and presenting to audiences all over the world in a sort of reverse engineering exercise, the pertinent question to ask is what we actually seek to enhance in an educational program through global connections. And the reason I have chosen to highlight our writing group is not related to any success story in itself, but rather in the joy derived by all of us in experiencing global education through our work that also entails a high degree of accomplishment in terms of our job satisfaction.

In the following sections, I will attempt to formulate some of the educational principles that should underpin any efforts at establishing global connections, both with the view that they do constitute meaningful and relevant education experiences for the students involved, as well as an often overlooked dimension of these initiatives, their sustainability. Unfortunately, and again, it is the nature of such projects, the rush with which educators have jumped into these projects has resulted in that a very high proportion of them are ephemeral, and in not providing students with continuity, may even send a counterproductive message in that they can be looked back upon as emerging and extraordinary, and not, as the intention should be, the norm in schooling.

Increase Cultural Awareness

How do we go about establishing sustainable global connections? The first answer that comes to mind is to increase cultural awareness for our students. Increasing our students' knowledge about the world, the way people live in different cultures, the existence and importance of local cultures, their traditions, habits, beliefs, behaviors, and anything else that can broaden the worldview of our students will undoubtedly help them in the irreversibly globalized world.

The most important outcome of such initiatives is related to overcoming any potential preconceptions, prejudices, or any other form of intolerance. It is needless to point out how racism, ethnic conflicts, religious hatred, and sadly, many other such manifestations have resulted in violence and wars. If anything, the 21st century interconnected world should be a catalyst for a better understanding between peoples of different geographical origins, races, and religions, and a platform to decisively overcome ancestral biases. Cultural biases may be inherent to the human condition, but the goal of education should be to bring these biases to light and examine them critically rather than accepting them as givens.

There are multiple dimensions of this challenge, including: celebrating diversity, embracing a truly multicultural setting, and viewing the differences of others as opportunities to enrich our own culture and perception of reality. When building sustainable global connections, the goal of increasing and deepening our cultural awareness should always be first and foremost in the planning of any educational endeavor.

Understand the Complexity and Possibilities of a Global World

This objective entails that students are able to reflect upon issues such as

- Their own role in the globalized world
- Challenges and opportunities of a world that allows infinite input and that provides an unlimited audience
- How the collective efforts of multicultural and multinational teams can pool their areas of expertise and their geographical and cultural advantages for increased and improved efficiency
- How colleagues from disparate contexts can be resources as well as potential recipients and clients of global initiatives
- The economic balance (or lack thereof) in the world
- The digital divide which separates the world into those who are connected to the Internet and those who are not, and the lack of opportunities that implies
- Technology tools that allow multinational collaboration, which emerge at a frenetic pace that challenges global users to discern what best serves the purpose of a project or problem to be solved

Be Agile

An important byproduct of global initiatives and exposing students to very different cultures is the realization that, in the global world, remaining rigidly affixed to a narrow horizon results inevitably in limited opportunities for the future. In contrast, being agile in expanding one's thoughts, goals, visions, and interpretations of reality allows each individual to realize increased opportunities for intellectual pursuits, career goals, business endeavors, and personal connections. The objective of building global connections is that students are no longer afraid or hesitant regarding that which is extraneous or foreign, and that they become prepared to seize opportunities even if those opportunities involve travel or settling in another culture.

✓ Move Toward a Worldview of Opportunities

Another significant dimension of establishing global connections involves moving away from a deficit model toward a worldview of opportunities. Often rhetoric has been centered on whether people in other countries will steal jobs from developed countries through outsourcing. This threatening discourse has done a lot of harm by presenting young people with a doomsday scenario that can prevent them from recognizing the world of possibilities opened up by the globalization process.

Instead, we should encourage students to embrace the potential of globalization for unlimited opportunities. Rather than looking for all we have to lose in the leveled playing field, we should recognize instead how we can seize the chances to establish long-lasting connections that will open doors for learning, expanded knowledge of products and services, the solving of problems, and hitherto impossible multicultural and long-distance friendships.

STRATEGIES FOR ESTABLISHING SUSTAINABLE GLOBAL CONNECTIONS

Below are suggested actions and schoolwide mechanisms to develop sustainable global connections, to favor an international mindset that will transcend isolated initiatives, to foster an atmosphere where global connections are a seamless part of everyday life, and to create a culture where students are able to intuitively relate to a world of unlimited opportunities.

In the Classroom

Include International Contents Within Subjects

Require international references for all assignments in all subject matters in a way that gets students used to reading about and learning from other cultures. This entails a conscious effort on the part of teachers to look out for opportunities to reframe assignments, projects, and evaluations in ways that allows students to gradually develop a sort of intercultural sixth sense that becomes immune to preconceptions and embraces differences as opportunities for growth.

Some examples could be

- A technology project that requires students to use presentation or publishing software to prepare a report on a country, its culture, traditions, and attractions
- An earth science assignment that deals with some process like erosion or natural disasters and utilizes as examples phenomena that have happened in other countries and how they have been approached and affected the local population.
- A science problem that is set in a real-life international location; for example, when studying free fall, the question can be about how long a diver takes to hit the water in one of the famous cliffs of Acapulco.
- Social studies assignments that require searching for current news and events in other countries that will illuminate and add nuance to the current topic

Shift Emphasis to an Expanded Worldview

Redesign the curriculum to explicitly address an international mindset.

Some suggested ideas as to how to approach this strategy would be:

- Integrate sources, Internet links, and even textbooks that are authored by international authors and that bring a different perspective to the subject at hand.
- Shift emphasis from remembering information to understanding the context, and making explicit links to what was happening at the time in other parts of the world. This is especially applicable to the social sciences.
- Move away from a superficial recounting of circumstances or geographical characteristics of other countries to a more thought-out analysis of global perspective. Require students to explore how people in other countries perceive, or react, and how their traditions shape them.
- Search for opportunities in all subjects to make crosslinks to international connections, comparisons, timelines, and other mechanisms to gain a wider perspective of what is being studied.
- Extend the scope of the curriculum, particularly in geography and history, to incorporate the study of as many other countries as possible; always from the perspective of going as deep as possible into the circumstances and perspectives of people who live in those countries.

Increase Students' Level of Awareness Regarding Globalization

Take advantage of every opportunity to discuss globalization, its implications, and the unlimited opportunities of a flat world, the equally divisive inequalities that prevent a really leveled playing field, the problem that every global citizen faces defining their own niche in the globalized world, and any other related theme that will serve to have our students become more enlightened regarding the promise and the challenges of globalization.

- Make sure that students are aware of international events, conflicts, economic trends, political changes, etc.
- Read foreign newspapers as a way to gain further insights into life in other countries, for example, have groups

within the classroom each adopt a country and then share their findings via a presentation with the rest of the class.

✓ • Review some of the many TED talks the deal with international conflicts, and which feature international presenters who share through testimonials some of the problems they face in their countries of origin and the creative solutions they have endeavored in order to solve them.

✓ • Develop the habit of leading class discussions about the role of a particular country in the world concert, strengths and weaknesses, opportunities, and in general, any discussion that targets developing a critical attitude toward globalization as a phenomenon.

✓ Lead Virtual International Trips

If budget does not allow for physical travel, Google Earth and many other wonderful tools allow for desktop exploration, that is, for teachers and students to be able to immerse themselves in different countries and undergo virtual trips that can span several lessons and become as in depth as the teacher requires. Even though they are no direct substitute for the real thing, the 3D photorealistic environments that are now available through computers can help bridge the distances and provide students with a genuine glimpse of what things look like at a different environment.

This seemingly trivial exercise can, indeed, yield very valuable results when analyzed from a genuinely interested point of view trying to unravel of some of the signs that can be read through these images and that can provide a knowledgeable cultural glimpse into everyday life in other places.

✓Encourage Participation in International Projects

There are a wide variety of organizations that host contests and other initiatives that foster globalization and allow students to reach out and work with their peers from all over the world. Many of these projects target different grade levels and open up significant opportunities for students to interact with their peers from all over the world. Some examples include:

- *International CyberFair:* Into its 18th year, this annual contest showcases Web-based projects from students all over the world in eight categories. After publishing their own projects, students are asked to conduct peer reviews of other projects from fellow participants, thus learning, in the process, about the issues and problems that other communities are dealing with (http://globalschoolnet .org/gsncf).
- *My Hero:* A project that seeks to highlight the potential of individuals to change the world through their collective contributions. Students can create and share their inspirational stories with children from all over the world (http://myhero.com).
- *World Wise Schools:* A website that features cross cultural materials and classroom activities based on Peace Corps experiences (http://peacecorps.gov/wws).
- *RoundSquare:* A worldwide association of schools sharing common values and working on community projects (http://roundsquare.org).
- *The Jason Project:* One of the oldest Web-based collaborative projects, The Jason Project connects students from classrooms worldwide to real scientific research, generally undertaken via field trips to remote locations (http://jason.org).
- *Journey North:* Defined as "A Global Study of Wildlife Migration and Seasonal Change," Journey North features student reports of sightings of animals related to migratory movements (http://learner.org/jnorth/maps/Gallery.html).

A Web search can yield innumerable other projects that cater to different subject matters and grade levels, so that teachers can find the best match. These easy to implement Web-based projects and contests should become commonplace in the school year, so that their value stems not only from the learning experience per se but also in having students acquire the habit of engaging in global collaborative activities as a habitual component of the learning process.

In the School

✓ Emphasize the Learning of Foreign Languages in the Curriculum

A truly fundamental way of fostering sustainable global connections and fueling the intrinsic motivation to try to reach out to different cultures is to learn foreign languages. A school curriculum that includes as many options as possible for students to learn and practice foreign languages will undoubtedly instill in them the desire to seek out these connections and, even, when possible, to travel abroad.

Many times, the greatest barrier to the implementation of such foreign language programs is the absence of a competent teacher and, understandably, the expense involved, especially when the number of students that have opted to study a particular foreign language is not very high. A way around this difficulty is the purchasing of specialized language-learning software, which have substantially increased their capabilities and become interactive immersive experiences that achieve a high degree of success in terms of language proficiency. To supplement this option, there are also wide variety of options in terms of online language learning courses that now include live interactions with instructors.

✓ International Diploma

Some schools have successfully implemented a sort of international roadmap that allows students to gain an international diploma when they graduate. Being able to be recognized as an international graduate often implies complying with a certain number of foreign language courses, having traveled abroad for a certain period of time, taking part in exchange trips, and other globalization-related curricular options that students can take in order to be awarded this international diploma.

✓ Implement Student Exchange Programs

A long-standing tradition in many schools, and one that has yielded valuable learning experiences, is the development of exchange trips that involve students spending a certain period

✓   of time visiting other schools, being students there, whilst, before or after, receiving their counterparts at home for a similar amount of time.

The value of such initiatives is related to the fact that students who go to a school abroad and live with foreign families experience a real-life immersion into that culture and country, which far transcends the tourist experience.

The main expense associated with such trips has to do with air tickets. The cost of living in a foreign country is much attenuated by the fact that the students stay with host families and most of their meals and expenses are taken care of. Student can finance their trips through fundraisers, summer jobs, and other means to attain their goal of traveling abroad.

In turn, when foreign students attend the school, the benefit extends to all the students in the school who have the opportunity to interact and learn from the exchange student. Being able to relate to them in a natural way is an integral part of the learning experience to sustaining global connections.

Some of the time, work, and expense of these exchange programs can be lessened by offering exchanges for shorter periods of time, that is, 2 weeks or a month, during school breaks. These programs are almost cost-free, and the school only needs to appoint staff members to take a part-time role in organizing the program, coordinating with host and foreign families, and following up on students who are doing the exchanges.

OVERCOMING CHALLENGES

Although we should, of course, focus more on the positives than the negatives, it is also useful to mention some of the challenges faced when trying to establish global connections and some of the most common pitfalls be avoided. It is important to stress that it is our role as educators to not just pay lip service to the concept of globalization and to be aware of the risks of not following up on initiatives. The sustainable dimension of the globalized initiatives is tremendously significant; otherwise, we may generate in the students a sort of ingrained skepticism about the impact of globalization in today's and the future world.

Here is a list of things to avoid:

- Don't focus only on food and costumes. Even though they are well-meaning initiatives, most of the programs that are carried out at schools focus on some of the more cosmetic aspects of the culture, the ones that are also more appealing and that enter through the eye and mouth perspective, that is, colorful typical garb associated with the culture of the country. This approach barely scratches the surface of the deep cultural traditions that are associated with different peoples and reinforces a rather shallow conception of what globalization entails. This by no means precludes showcasing local food and traditional attire, but if this is done, we need to make sure that there and enough background materials explaining the reason for the wearing of these clothes, what they represent, in what historic events and traditions they are based, why certain food is produced and consumed in the country, related to their geographic and economic conditions; that is, make sure that these outward manifestations of a culture that are easily discernible and understood serve as a gateway for a deeper understanding of the cultural heritage that is portrayed by them.
- Don't organize Skype connections without any educational objective. While these may allow students the opportunity to communicate with their counterparts from different places in the world, the lack of a defined sense of purpose ensures that these connections are short-lived and not sustainable over time. The implicit message is that these connections are extraordinary events in the school year. In contrast, aim to build sustainable connections that involve working and collaborating with other schools in different parts of the world as a normal and regular part of the school day. These connections need to be supported by some substantive

work that does not stray away from the school curriculum and that also takes advantage of the point of view of the other school.

- Don't offer one-way, expensive service trips. Although these trips have yielded great benefits to the communities they have served, unwittingly, they may reinforce cultural biases. Nobody can deny the positive impact of trips where students help out in service projects or deliver essential supplies and medicines, but very often students are only exposed to one reality without truly understanding the cultural complexities that have led to the humanitarian crisis in the first place. These one-off trips sometimes mean that students are missing out on very important opportunities to relate to their peers in those countries on an even playing field. Often the costs involved far outweigh the amount spent on providing the service. In most places, students can potentially address humanitarian crises in their local communities. By traveling far away to "exotic" destinations students are in a way being blinded to seeing and acknowledging the needs of their local communities. It seems much more useful to work on an ongoing project collaboratively with foreign students, for example, to devise an inexpensive water purifying device that can be used to stop infant mortality due to contaminated water rather than spending thousands of dollars transporting loads of students to paint walls in a village in that same community. If trips are to be conducted at all, they should entail interactions between young people from both communities in ways that ensure that the students who do the service learning work are also recipients and benefit and grow from their interaction with their peers. Otherwise, the message that is being passed along is that the relation is asymmetrical and that the more materially wealthy communities are the ones who give and the poor are the ones who receive, when, what we seek to accomplish is a broader worldview where we can all learn from each other regardless of differences in economic power.

The guiding principles for sustainable global connections call out for legitimate genuine interactions, that are dealt with as naturally as possible, and that allow students to gain a broader perspective that leads to a better understanding of other peoples as well as an increased knowledge and awareness of opportunities to be gained in the global marketplace.

REFLECTION: THINK GLOBAL, ACT LOCAL

One of the universally accepted mantras regarding globalization has to do with this idea of thinking globally and acting locally, and it leads to an interesting question regarding the extent to which these globalization initiatives should be implemented at the school level. The main concern whenever authors and thinkers call for a more globalized school is related to the lack of focus, losing sight of the national and local identity by virtue of a stronger emphasis on looking abroad. Some of the more conservative voices would say that young people need to reinforce their convictions, relate to their local cultural traditions, and that exposing them to too many extraneous cultures could result in a feeling of uncertainty that may leave many young people unsettled and vulnerable to external influences that are alien to who they are.

This is a false dichotomy. The whole idea of thinking globally but acting locally represents an answer in itself: Broadening our worldview, learning more about other cultures, understanding other cultures better should become a platform for a better perspective on who we are ourselves. Part of the challenge for young people in this fascinating and yet tantalizing challenge that they face in the globalized interconnected world is finding their own place, their own spot in the increasingly leveled playing field. Being able to do so entails understanding who they are, reinforcing our local and culture that entity, evaluating our competitive advantages and gaining a greater sense of awareness of how from our own back yard we can contribute to the infinite globalized world.

In order to do this, it is very important that throughout the whole development of globalization related projects some elements be included to allow students to express their own local cultures, so that, on the one hand, they directly help their counterparts to learn more about their own particular country or region, but also as a way to affirm that working in a global context does not erase the local identities, but rather enhances them through contributing from each school's in countries original richness.

We are sad witnesses to many governments that instill in their citizens a fear of foreign cultures that borders on the paranoid and results, inevitably, in contexts that very well end up escalating into full-fledged wars. It cannot be stressed enough how important it is to have young students learn from a very early age that cultural differences are to be celebrated, and that nothing is lost learning more about other cultures, sharing with them, and enjoying a broader perspective. Outdated nationalistic views are still very much a threat in today's world. Therefore, doing away with cultural bigotry and prejudice is one of the most important spinoffs of global sustainable connections.

ACTIVITY #1: DEVELOP A SUSTAINABLE LEARNING PROJECT WITH A CLASSROOM ABROAD

Participants: Teachers from at least two different cultures and their students

Objective: To provide an opportunity for students to communicate with, collaborate with, and learn from their peers in a disparate locale and to share in the learning process on a global platform.

Process (takes place over the academic year):

Find a Common Topic in the Curriculum

Teachers can exchange their respective unit plans so as to find a topic or unit where they match. The next step involves seeing if the scope and sequence of the teaching and learning of those units can be coordinated so that both schools can cover same topics concurrently.

✓ *Develop a Common Assignment*

Create an assignment that is exactly the same for students in both or more schools. Develop a shared rubric so that students will be assessed in the same way. Ensure that even if there are differences in the grading system, grades are based on the same criteria. Assign groups so that half of your students belong to each of the schools. Decide on a common series of deadlines and milestones for the project development. Allow students to interact in whatever way they please when they collaborate on their joint assignment since it is part of the learning process that students make the best use of existing social networks or other means of communication to achieve the desired objectives.

Elements for a Successful Global Project

✓ *Select a Topic That can be Enriched by the Diverse Perspectives*

Ask, Why would we do this project with students from the school in a different place in the world? Reflecting on this question should help ensure that the project is meaningful to all the students involved. Aim to avoid the message that the project is being done just of the sake of doing it, reinforcing the idea that globalization is an artificial construct. Relevant tasks or components might involve, for example, students taking measurements in their respective geographical locations or analyzing perspectives and variables from the other community, taking photographs or reviewing particular elements of their culture, and so on. The work of the students should benefit from having data or analysis by students from another school.

Include a Cultural Component

Require students to incorporate a cultural flavor that reflects their own place in the community and that asserts their community identity in the face of globalization. Whenever possible, the project should have ramifications that extend into their local cultures so that they are able to make explicit references to the local culture as a way for the other students to learn more about their community and, also very important, so that students can revisit and reflect on their own distinctive cultural traits.

Be Presented Jointly

Ensure that students from the disparate locales have the space and time to present the results of their work together to one audience. The presentation or work should be graded collaboratively by both teachers. Ideally, the global collaborative project should continue throughout the academic year, where the respective curriculums are evenly matched and activities can be done in the most unobtrusive way, so that gradually, they are no longer a novelty, but rather a habitual way of work, so as to make the idea of working collaboratively with their peers and their globalized world more natural.

Reflection: Have students share with their peers locally and abroad what they learned over the course of the year-long project.

Activity #2: Design a Product That Can Be Sold in a Foreign Market

Participants: Students

Objective: Students will have the opportunity to look at the world as a global marketplace rather than limiting their viewpoint to their local market. They will gain a greater awareness of cultural traditions in the designated country, and an inside view of another culture.

Process

- Think of a product that can satisfy a need in a foreign market.
  - Research market conditions in a foreign country, specifically what market needs there might be in that

economy in terms of unsatisfied demand or find a foreign market where there are opportunities based on the favorable exchange rate, possibilities for out-sourcing, or particular needs that can be satisfied by a product that they can develop locally.

○ Learn the habits and cultural traditions of the country; find out what goods and services are consumed there; find out which goods and services are in high demand and supply.

• Design a product based on the research conducted in Step 1.

Next Steps: Design and plan for a version of the product to sell in other markets. Research costs and prices. Come up with a plan to produce and export. Calculate the cost of transportation, restrictions to trade, etc.

6

Global Competencies and Citizenship

by Emily McCarren

"Human beings face tremendous challenges: environmental degradation; drastic climate change; natural disasters; large and small conflicts among national, ethnic and religious groups; hunger and poverty; energy; health; aging; migration; and unemployment to name just a few. These challenges are global problems intensified by globalization. . . . Being able to adopt a perspective that helps to examine these problems as rich opportunities for new products and services is what is needed for global business entrepreneurs, social entrepreneurs and policy entrepreneurs."

—Zhao (2012, p. 223)

Featured School

Lakeside School, Seattle, WA

The Lakeside School, an independent school in Seattle, Washington, made a strong commitment to developing global citizens, a commitment demonstrated in the school's renowned Global Service Learning (GSL; n.d.) programs. These programs allow high school students to travel to one of the school's nine sites globally and participate in service-learning projects in a culturally immersive environment. These month-long programs are preceded by 5 days of preparation at the school on the outskirts of Seattle. All of the programs include home-stay experiences and the opportunity to make meaningful contributions to communities globally.

Charlotte Blessing, Lakeside's Director of Global Education, reflects on the importance of engaging the students in meaningful work, by contributing to communities through their real expertise and passion to share. For example, Lakeside students developed an art workshop for the local community, sharing their skills and creating art and shared expression with the members of the global community. Students with expertise in athletics found it meaningful to share those skills in the form of sports camps at the GSL sites globally. Each year at Lakeside, between 60% and 80% of the graduating class has participated in one of the Global Service Learning experiences at some point in their high school career. The school uses funds from its endowment to subsidize the cost of the program for each student, and provides financial assistance to families for whom even the highly subsidized cost is out of reach.

The school is launching the Global Service Learning program for its middle school students this year—it will allow students in the eighth grade to participate in an experience in the Pacific Northwest that focuses on issues at the intersection of economy, environment, and culture in their region. This program will prime the eighth graders to consider the local contexts of their global learning that will follow in their high school years.

In addition to these remarkable programs for students, each year Lakeside sends a small group of teachers to one of the sites for a week of the students' month-long program—to be with the students, participate in the service, experience the place, and meet people. Blessing tells the

(Continued)

(Continued)

teachers their most important job is to hear the students, to listen and learn and gain a deeper understanding of the learning experience students are a part of. This practice helps grow the program and encourages faculty to lead GSL trips. It also contributes to creating a culture on the campus back in Seattle that shares the beliefs about the value of the work they and the students are doing. And GSL faculty and students help create an urgency to connect their experiences to the curriculum.

At Lakeside, service in the global context is the means for cultural immersion and development of global competencies. The belief that students can do meaningful work in the world, and not just prepare to do it after their schooling is over, is the hallmark of these programs. This chapter will explore the notion of global competencies and developing global citizens through schooling and introduce a framework that will help everyone in a school community to contribute to this effort.

PRINCIPLES FOR DEVELOPING GLOBAL CITIZENS

- Look in
- Look out
- Bring in
- Go out
- Create together and work with

Arriving at a definition of global competencies and understanding the meaning of global citizenship can feel like an unwieldy task for schools. Even more complex is the work of incorporating these concepts in the work we do in classrooms. This chapter will present a framework to facilitate this work in schools so that all of our students have the opportunity to develop these competencies, allowing them to be meaningful participants in their communities around the world.

As discussed in World Class Learners, practitioners and scholars have tried for some time to define global citizenship and tease out the competencies schools should instill to prepare students for meaningful engagement as global citizens. Agreement has been elusive, even as consensus grows that preparation of global citizens is an increasingly essential component of the work we do in schools. Since the 1940s, it has been declared in each decade that now is the time to focus on global education. And here, well into the second decade of the 21st century, the claim is still strong—*now* is the time.

While there are exciting examples of schools that have been founded with the focus on global education (Think Global, Avenues), what do we say to existing schools that don't have the benefit of a clean slate like a start-up? How can those schools begin to understand that the work of global competencies and graduating global citizens is the responsibility and domain of every teacher in the school? To be successful, all members of the school community have to understand and be committed to this common goal of nurturing global citizens.

One of the most compelling voices in this field is Professor Fernando Reimers of the Harvard Graduate School of Education. He asserts that the factors in global citizenship are

- A capacity to understand the world and to function globally
- Intercultural competency
- World language skills
- Knowledge of world history
- An understanding of globalization (Walsh & Webber, 2015)

Some of these factors (languages, world history, and geography, even globalization) are common in most K–12 schools' curricula, and even part of most national curricula globally. But what about "intercultural competency," or a "capacity to understand the world and to function globally"? Schools need concrete ways to understand how to encourage these, and all teachers, not just the language and social studies teachers in high schools, need to see that as an important part of their work.

One of the challenges to creating a schoolwide commitment to global education is that it is often compartmentalized in different subject areas. In middle and secondary schools, language teachers and social studies departments sometimes decide this is their job. But it is not one department's work; it is everyone's job.

This framework provides a way for everyone in a school, from the kindergarten teachers, to coaches, to staff members, to understand how the work they are doing fits into the greater goal of preparing global citizens.

The framework covers five areas:

1. Look in

2. Look out

3. Bring in

4. Go out

5. Create together and work with

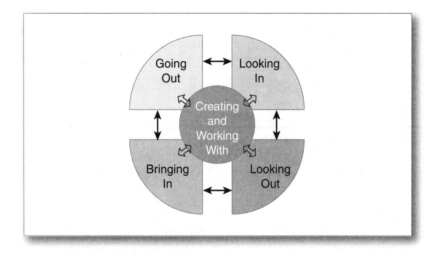

This framework distills the complex nuances of global competencies into types of learning experiences that students will build on over their careers in school. This learning is multifaceted, and it is not just a topic or content area to be "covered" in one specific class. Rather, a student's learning and development as a global citizen is about a mindset to be developed over time. Global citizenship is a rippling out of understandings; first you learn about yourself and your own small sphere of experience. And then you explore increasingly greater circles of understanding and finally move on to shared learning and meaning making—learning with and not just about people from other communities globally. This framework is not a lock step progression; it is something that students (and faculty) will cycle through in different age-appropriate ways throughout their schooling.

Look In

An essential foundation of a well-educated global citizen is a strong sense of self and understanding of one's place in the world. Before anyone can begin to function in a multicultural environment, they must be able to understand their own culture and community, and also their own desires, needs, and identity. In the long road to global citizenship, first comes an understanding of self, and the customs and cultures of your home, family, and community. This is common in an early childhood curriculum: How do I describe myself? What are my wishes? Who is my family? What does my community look like? And anyone who has taught secondary school knows that these essential questions are also the domain of high school courses in many subjects. This exploration of the self is foundational in developing global citizens and is best facilitated as a series of developmentally appropriate tasks over the entire course of a student's school, career, and life. The reflection involved in looking in is something to which students and the people who guide their learning should continue to return throughout the schooling experience.

Look Out

As students begin to know themselves better, they can begin to understand that, all around the world, there are people experiencing their own realities in different, but fundamentally similar ways. This opening up to the rest of the world begins as early as kindergarten (or before for many students) and continues in different ways until they graduate. This is the "look out" element of the work, where we hope that students develop reflexes of empathy and nonjudgmental curiosity about the world. You need to know some things about other parts of the world, other cultures, their history, and their reality. And in many global education programs, this is where it stops. Students, in their walled classrooms, learn about other places through textbooks and static media. Even schools with robust global citizenship tracks can tend to overemphasize this part of the framework. Most social studies courses and elements of world language courses that deal with people and culture are situated squarely in the "look out" category. An increased depth of understanding will be brought to learning when this is combined with other levels of the framework. (See the "In the School or District Level" section in this chapter for thoughts on this.)

Bring In

One simple way to expand students' awareness of cultural diversity is to have guests come to class and school. Around the world, there are countless guests in schools every day (virtually or in person), representing different viewpoints, cultures, and places. Including different voices in the classroom increases motivation and readiness for students to do more meaningful investigations in their looking out and also nurtures a more careful looking in, illuminating the things that make them and their home cultures more interesting, unique, and meaningful. This can also go poorly, if a visitor or guest speaker doesn't know how to connect with a group, or delivers content that is not engaging or appropriate; students can become disengaged (at best) or begin to use stereotypes to understand.

Go Out

And then there is going out. This could be out of the classroom, to a museum, to a performance in town, a walk through a local ethnic neighborhood, or a travel opportunity to another country for a month, semester, or year. This has long been a hallmark of global education programs, and many consider this to be the pinnacle, the ultimate global experience. To go and live in a place can certainly be a meaningful experience. And, it can be argued that you can travel to a place and not have a true "going out" experience. If you go to a country and visit just the spots where the guidebooks send you, speak only to your travel companions or other Americans, and eat only at restaurants where you can read the menu, then perhaps you have not really given your all to the experience, and will not be rewarded in the same ways.

The research behind the notion of "getting out of your comfort zone" and why it is good for learning is related to a concept called "the zone of proximal development" (ZPD), first described by Vygotzky (Hedegaard, 2005). This theoretical framework is borrowed from the field of psychology and describes how learning happens best at the edge between where you are comfortable and where you are challenged. As a learner, if things are too easy, you will likely not progress too far. And you won't get too far if things are completely over your head. The sweet spot is that place where students are just at the edge of uncomfortable, and yet able to feel success in what they are doing. The implication for this in teaching is that if the instruction is aimed too far behind the ZPD, the child will be bored, and disengage; if aimed too far in front, the child will feel like he or she doesn't know what's going on, get frustrated and disengage. And a neat thing about this research is that it shows that as students progress, that zone moves with them (further support for the call to personalize student's learning; a standardized curriculum is unlikely to be precisely in any one student's zone of proximal development).

This concept of "going out" is based on this idea of moving kids beyond their comfort zones. We have to take our students to places, into experiences, in which they are not totally comfortable so that they can learn, and learn to be themselves in new environments. This is one of the important foundations of global citizenship.

Create Together and Work With

Look in, look out, bring in, and go out form the frame of our work. Many careful efforts to cultivate global competencies don't go beyond these first four elements of the global competency framework. For many schools, the idea of "go out" is the unreachable element of the developing global competencies—all educators, even those at schools like Lakeside, wish there were a way for even more students to have the global experiences afforded by a thoughtful program like Lakeside's GSL. But even thoughtful global learning programs that involve travel to far-flung places are not the pinnacle of developing global citizens. The key is not travel; the key is the final element of the framework: creating together and working with.

This piece brings together several elements of the World Class Learning paradigm, personalized, product-oriented learning in a global space. And it is key to know that this does not have to be something that, like the GSL programs at Lakeside school, send students out into the world—technology can effectively mediate this co-creation. By leveraging technology, teachers in schools of very little means can create highly meaningful opportunities for their students to create and work with students from other parts of the world. The essential question here is how do we get our students doing their meaningful work with (and not just for) other students around the world that serves positive social good? With a little bit of creativity and flexibility, this can be the work of every teacher.

In a school where everyone sees this as their responsibility, starting in kindergarten, we can expect to see students developing the global competencies that we aspire to for our students by giving them the opportunities to connect with other people and co-create experiences and projects that have meaning.

This five-element framework can be molded to fit the needs of any school. Each school or district can work independently to define (or choose a definition) of global competencies for developing global citizens that works best for the particular community. Then, they can go about validating the good work that so many of their teachers are doing by connecting different efforts to this framework.

Strategies for Developing Global Citizens

In the Classroom

Include Authentic Voices (Thinking: Beginning)

Starting as early as the elementary grades and on through middle school and high school, make it a habit to include the "bring in" element of the global citizenship framework in your classes. You could have a "guest of the week" or "guest of the month." This outside voice can be someone from the community that can physically come to your classroom, or you can Skype with people from all over the world to help bring diverse voices to your class. When people join you in your class, have a series of questions that you always ask, and also allow the students to write questions ahead of time. Encourage inquiry about cultural viewpoints and value systems, as appropriate to the visitor and setting.

Require Global Collaboration (Expanding: Advanced)

At the middle and high school level, instead of having collaborative projects within a class, join forces with another teacher and form groups across schools in different parts of the world. The National Association of Independent Schools in the United States supports a project called the 20/20 Challenge, open to all schools (public, independent, international), which pairs schools together to work on pressing issues outlined in the book *High Noon: 20 Global Problems, 20 Years to Solve Them* (2003) by Jean Francois Rischard. This program connects schools looking to address these problems; it costs nothing for participating schools and requires no travel.

Create Rubrics That Prize Global
Collaboration and Connection (Expanding: Advanced)

In a middle or high school class, in your project rubrics for assessment, include an element that prizes and rewards global collaboration. A high school Spanish teacher made one of the elements of getting A (the top mark in the class) possible only if students demonstrated that their work included "meaningful collaboration with people currently living in the Spanish-speaking world outside of the United States." This open-end challenge resulted in students Skyping with family friends living abroad to learn about their experiences, engaging in interesting dialogue on Twitter about the Arab Spring, and co-producing a cooking blog with a student at a partner school in Ecuador. Although we don't want grades to be the motivator for anything in our classrooms, if we deeply value the notion of "creating and working with" as the most powerful way to develop the global competencies that we prize in our schools, then our assessment systems should reflect this value. Also, if students are being challenged to connect outside of the classroom walls to do their work, it will be essential that teachers are doing the important work of teaching students how to establish and work effectively in global teams. A good resource for this is the work of Julie Lindsay (n.d.) in the Flat Connections Network.

"Create and Work With" at the
Class Level in the Co-curricular (Intermediate)

Sometimes, there is a good reason for a class to engage in a particular project as a larger group and not as individuals. Perhaps it is a class that doesn't meet often enough to have sufficient time for deeply personalized curriculum, or a course where the teacher has too many students to be able to support a highly individualized curriculum. But that does not mean that "creating and working with" can't happen in these courses, too. For example, in many high schools, the music, art and physical education teachers have a higher average student load than many of the other teachers. As a music teacher, you could partner with a teacher in another country and create a virtual concert (see Eric Whitacre's [n.d.] Virtual Choir for inspiration). You could have a performance of two songs, one written by your school and performed by your partner school, and one written by your partner school and performed by your school.

In a Physical Education class, you could arrange a Skype session with another school and exchange presentations about your favorite sports, and then try out those sports in class the next day. In an Art course, you could study the art or national treasures of a community and have your students prepare questions about the work and why it is seen as important for a class in another country, and vice versa. Also, you could create virtual galleries of work inspired by the work that your partner class describes to you and then share in a virtual space where students can leave each other reflections and feedback.

In the School or District Level

Develop or Join a Consortium of Schools
Looking at Global Issues (Beginning to Advanced)

There are a number of established programs schools or districts can join or participate in that are focused on developing global citizens, and in particular on supporting schools in the complicated "creating together and working with" part of the framework described in this chapter. An example is the Global Issues Network (GIN; n.d.), which like NAIS's Project 20/20 was conceived based on the work of Rischard's book *High Noon: 20 Global Problems and 20 Years to Solve Them.* The hallmark of the GIN is student conferences that happen all over the world and focus on intense collaboration. If travel is not possible for your school, consider finding a virtual group to join; an example is the Flat Connection network.

If there isn't a network or established organization in place that makes sense for your school community and culture, find eager and energetic teachers or students who are passionate about the cause of developing global citizenship and challenge them to develop opportunities for your students.

Assess the Global Competencies of
Students at Your School (Beginning-Intermediate)

There are a number of validated instruments for measuring global competencies at the K–12 level. Consider finding one that would work for your school and assess your students longitudinally to see what impact your school program has on global competencies (as defined by at least one of the assessments). One instrument is the Global Competence Aptitude Assessment (GCAA). The GCAA website (n.d.) defines global competency as "Having an open mind while actively seeking to understand cultural norms and expectations of others, and leveraging this gained knowledge to interact, communicate, and work effectively in diverse environments." This test measures internal and external readiness to be successful in a diverse environment. Internal readiness is related to the "look in" part of the framework discussed in this chapter and is about knowing yourself and your own culture. Also, it is about an individual's disposition and reactions to and interactions with other cultures and people. And it concerns skills and competencies developed in everything from the "bring in" to the "create with." The external competencies deal with the knowledge of world history and geography (languages are not measured in this test). What the results often show in traditional schools in the United States is that schools do a much better job growing students' external readiness, but have little impact on their internal readiness. Gaining a better understanding of the current reality in your school would be a great start to initiating meaningful change in the curriculum.

REFLECTION: WHY WE
WANT TO TAKE ON THE CHALLENGE

If we are to realize the vision of creating opportunities for our students to become World Class Learners, teachers and school leaders must bring global competencies and the development of global citizens to the core of our work. We have to be unforgiving in making time and space to think about this and insist that our students have the same kinds of opportunities to develop these competencies as they do those traditionally prized in schools.

The good news is that if our schools are primed to do this work—using the affirming framework of look in, look out, bring in, go out, and create with—we will find that this is the shared work of many in our schools, and there is much good work we are already doing. World Class Learners need to be ready today to do the good work that they are drawn to, not just prepared to do good work later in life. Developing global citizens is the most complex and the most important work that we do.

ACTIVITY #1: LOOKING AT OUR WORK THROUGH A GLOBAL COMPETENCIES LENS

Participants: Teachers, school administrative teams, district-level educators

Objective: The purpose of this activity is to reframe the work that our schools are already doing to validate educators and also to acknowledge that a shift in focus to emphasize global competencies and citizenship is not, actually, far off from what most schools are hoping to do. After this activity, participants should feel engaged in the shared work of developing global competencies and have a clear sense of what their role in this work is.

Materials

- Print copies of the framework on large (11x17) or tabloid size paper.
- Sticky notes
- Or, for digital version:
  - Wi-Fi
  - Have each participant have an image of the framework in a program (keynote, Powerpoint, Google

Presentations, etc. . . .) in which they can add labels then share with the group.

○ You might make a Google Presentation with the framework on the number of slides that you have participants and then label each slide with a person's name. Then when it is time to share, you can use one computer to flip through the slide show that was created by everyone.

Process

5 minutes: Group presentation on the framework

15 minutes: Have everyone work individually to add things (one sentence summary) that they do in their classes to each of the five parts of the framework.

5 minutes: Share everyone's work.

Reflection

Ask all groups to reflect on the activity.

What did they learn?

How might this knowledge affect their future practice?

Did the activity make you feel more engaged in the work of developing global competencies? Do you understand global competencies better now? Why or why not?

Do you have a clear sense of what your role is in developing global competencies in your students? How would you articulate that role?

ACTIVITY #2: CURRICULUM MAPPING USING THE GLOBAL COMPETENCIES FRAMEWORK

Participants: Grade-level leaders, department chairs, teachers, school administrative teams, district-level educators

Objective: The purpose of this activity is to support teachers and administrators in seeing where and how global competencies are being developed in your school or district.

Materials

- Copies of the Global Competencies Framework
- Large 6–15ft piece of butcher paper, or long white board for meeting #2
- Markers in five different colors (enough for the whole group)

Organization: Groups of two

Process: Two 20-minute meetings on different days

Meeting #1: Participants should be introduced to the Global Competencies Framework described in this chapter, or another framework that the school or district is using to describe their aspirations for the development of global citizens. Then, let the participants know that when they return for the second meeting, they will be asked to share where in the school these things are practiced.

Meeting #2: Hang butcher paper horizontally with grade levels of the school listed at the top of the paper throughout the length of the paper (Kindergarden, Grade 1, etc.). Determine which color will signify which part of the framework (looking in, looking out, etc.) and have participants use the colored markers to note the elements of what they do with their students that are described in the model. Alternately, this can poster can be left out in a shared space for teachers over a week so that people have time to fill in the paper. If you are a large school or district, you might pass the paper around from lounge to lounge and then come together to reflect and debrief what is shared.

Reflection

- What elements of the framework are most present in our students' experiences? Why might that be?
- Are there elements that are absent? Why?
- How might we have more of the "creating and working with" in our learning environments?
- What might the consequences be of not doing this?

Activity #3: What are my global competencies?

Participants: Students

Objective: The purpose of this activity is to empower students to celebrate and continue to develop their global competencies. This activity can be done in a standalone class, in an advisory session, or pretty much any subject area.

Materials

- None

Organization: Full class followed by individual work and reflection

Process (25+ minutes)

Introduction: Describe the global competencies that your school has defined as goals to the students. Or, if the school does not have any specific global competencies, use the framework described in this chapter or one of the many definitions that resonates with you as a teacher. Remind students that this is not a test, and that there are no good or bad answers, but just their own answers.

Interview: Have each of the students interview a partner about his or her global competencies. You can use some of the sample questions below, develop your own, or use questions from one of the global competency tests, such as the GCAA.

- What are your strengths in terms of global competencies?
- How well do you understand your own community? Explain.
- Do you know another community really well? Maybe another place where you or your family has lived?
- How would you describe your understanding of world history?

- In what languages can you communicate?
- When you hear people speaking a language that you don't understand, what is your reaction?

Reflection: Invite each student to write for 5 minutes on what they learned, how they are feeling, and what global competencies they might like to develop in the future, and why?

ACTIVITY #4: IMAGINING OUR PERFECT GLOBAL CITIZENS

Participants: Teachers and administrators

Objective: The purpose of this activity is to engage teachers and/or administrators in the work of visualizing the outcomes that the school desires in terms of developing global citizens. This activity can be part of a faculty meeting or a special task force or committee exploring global citizenship.

Materials

- Butcher paper (5-foot-long pieces, one for each group of three or four people)
- Markers
- Large tables or floor space to draw

Organization: Full group introduction (5 minutes); then break into groups of three to four (10 minutes); come back together to share and discuss (10–15 minutes).

Process (25+ minutes, depending on the size of the group): Invite participants to invent imaginary adults who have gone through your school and personify your goals of global competencies and citizenship. Encourage them to develop a story about their lives, who they are, what they have accomplished, where they live, what they are like, etc. Have each group draw a representation of this person (drawing skills are not important, just a way to free up thinking).

Post the following prompts if the group needs nudging to flesh out their imaginary alumni.

- What are their names?
- What has their career trajectory been?
- What do people notice about their work in their chosen field?
- Do they have children? Do they send their children to our school?
- What about their time at our school has impacted the choices they made in terms of how "global" they became?

Reflection

After the presentations are concluded, initiate discussion and reflection.

- Do participants notice anything about their sense of the work of developing global competencies in the school?
- How are we doing?
- What might we do more of or less of to further support the development of these ideal global citizens?

Next Steps

Find two to three alumni who actually personify the ideals of the school in terms of global citizens. Have a different faculty member connect with them via phone or Skype and conduct an interview that focuses on their experience of your school and what role they think the school played in preparing them for life. Have the teachers share 3-minute summaries of their conversations at the next faculty gathering or school board meeting.

REFERENCES

Global Issues Network. (n.d.). Retrieved from http://globalissues network.org/#

Global Competence Aptitude Assessment. (n.d.). Definition of global competence. Retrieved from http://www.globallycompetent.com/

Global Service Learning at Lakeside School. (n.d.). Retrieved from http://www.lakesideschool.org/GSL

Hedegaard, M. (2005). The zone of proximal development as basis for instruction. In H. Daniels (Ed.), *An introduction to Vygotsky* (2nd ed., p. 227). New York, NY: Routledge.

Lindsay, J. (n.d.). Flat connections. Retrieved from http://www.flatconnections.com/

NAIS 20/20 challenge. (n.d.). Retrieved from http://www.nais.org/Articles/Pages/Challenge-20-20.aspx

Rischard, J. (2003). *High Noon 20 global problems, 20 years to solve them.* New York, NY: Basic Books.

Walsh, B., & Webber, M. (2015). The global classroom: As the world grows more interconnected, education looks outward. Retrieved from https://www.gse.harvard.edu/news/uk/15/02/global-classroom

Whitacare, E. (n.d.). The virtual choir. Retrieved from http://ericwhitacre.com/the-virtual-choir

Building a
Global Campus

Costs and Infrastructure

by Emily McCarren

Oxford Community Schools, Oxford, Michigan

Oxford Community Schools (OCS) is a small school district located in a northern suburb of Detroit, about half way between Detroit and Flint. Michigan, and the Detroit area in particular, has experienced firsthand the dramatic conditions that call for the shift to a different kind of education. As the American auto industry evolved and outsourced to cheaper labor overseas, and the city filed for bankruptcy, it was clear that it was no longer enough to train workers, or even managers, for assembly-line type of work (McDonald, 2014). When OCS began its strategic planning process in 2008 (in the middle of a nationwide recession that was hitting Michigan and its industries particularly hard), there was already a clear sense that education needed to change. At that point, with a good deal of community input, OCS developed a bold and forward-facing mission statement: " . . . to provide a world-class education that challenges all students to achieve their maximum potential and prepares them to succeed in a global society," with a vision to create a "world-class education today to shape tomorrow's selfless global leaders."

Tim Throne has been working in OCS throughout that process and was appointed superintendent in the summer of 2014. The tagline for the district is, "Oxford Community Schools, where the globe is our campus" (OCS, n.d.). This is lofty language that indicates OCS has done a remarkable job—all of its schools, pre-K–12, boast the International Baccalaureate programs and degrees, something that represents a significant commitment for a public school district. The district has also committed itself to nurturing a few crucial international partnerships with schools in China and Mexico, which foster student, teacher, and administrator travel and exchanges. World languages are core, not elective, and are required for all students, from kindergarten through Grade 10. In addition, the district has an independently managed residential program for international students, and the mobility that the IB programs allow means that more students can come and go from the district, creating quite a cosmopolitan community in a small suburb of a city that is far from thriving.

Oxford has a particularly dense population of engineers, even for a state with the highest number of engineers per capita in the country (Center for Automotive Research, 2014). Superintendent Throne notes that parents of his students understand the need for a shift toward education in a global context: "I can't tell you how many of my parents have told me that core parts of their day are doing international business, being on international teams, and those are some of those skills that are hard to quantify on a standardized test, and yet are really important to employers when they go to hire people" (T. Throne. personal communication, July 27, 2015). OCS was part of a dramatically shifting landscape in an American city. They realized that there were intercultural and entrepreneurial skills and global competencies that were going to be needed in the evolving economy, and as Throne says, "We can either go out to find these people, or we can grow them here." The commitment to make large shifts in the school system has not been simple, but Throne insists that it was necessary, and now the community feels united in this important work of building global schools in service of students, the community, and their shared future.

PRINCIPLES FOR BUILDING A GLOBAL CAMPUS

- Take technology into consideration: Four factors
  - Connectivity
  - Accessibility
  - Legal considerations
  - Hardware

- Plan for globalness: Structures, staffing, and hiring
  - Lead toward the global campus
  - Hire for global mindedness
  - Provide professional development for teachers

Until relatively recently, the concept of a global campus has been out of reach for most primary and secondary schools because of the prohibitive cost of international travel. Economically feasible ways of connecting students to the rest of the world were limited to exchanging letters or other postal-based exchanges and perhaps the occasional international trip for a small portion of the student body. While the anticipation of getting a letter from a peer on the other side of the world has excited many a student over the years, it is an activity that seems to emphasize the distance and difference, as opposed to making students feel closer to their peers globally. Of course, now with the ubiquity of the Internet, the possibilities of student interaction are nearly limitless. Any classroom with at least one device (computer, phone, or tablet) connected to the Internet can become a continually globally connected space with the opportunity to leverage relationships to other teachers, schools, and off-campus experts. Also, it creates the opportunity for students to connect and engage with students in real time. There is a spectrum of connectivity here, from the very highly personalized (one or more devices per student) to the classroom based connectivity (one device per class), and that spectrum runs from the very costly to the frugal. However, with the right teacher at the helm, any situation can yield a fantastic learning environment for students.

There is a broad spectrum of ways in which schools and classes can become more globally connected—from technology, to partner school relationships, to globally based programs for students. This chapter will discuss some of the ways that school infrastructure can support the movement toward a global campus in both high- and low-tech ways. First, it will focus on the issues of technology for fostering global connections. Then, we will consider the ways that structures, staffing, and hiring can impact the globalness of a school, and finally, we will offer some further suggestions as to how (on a limited budget) schools can move toward their aspirations of a global campus.

Take Technology Into Consideration: Four Factors

The spectrum of technology integration in schools globally is extraordinary. From one-room school houses with no electricity to schools where every student carries around at least two Internet-accessible devices with him or her at all times, the range can be staggering. Despite the wide diversity, there are four key things for teachers and school leaders to consider in terms of technology infrastructure for their global classrooms and schools: connectivity, accessibility, legal considerations, and hardware.

Connectivity

The most important area of concern is Internet connectivity. While Internet connectivity may not be possible for all schools, it should be the primary area of opportunity for improvement in schools seeking to become globally connected. Internet connectivity is an essential foundation in World Class Learning environments. While there is something to be said for innovative programs, particularly in Africa, involving SMS as an educational platform, the Internet accessed through Web browsers and videoconferencing software is a remarkable tool for personalized, product-oriented, globally connected learning. Schools have a number of important considerations when outfitting their school with Internet access. When possible, they should seek to have sufficient bandwidth so that students and teachers can leverage video-conferencing tools without experiencing frustrating delays. Information technology (IT) administrators at the school should work closely with academic leadership to ensure that traffic to supported websites can be given priority access to the available broadband.

If the school has relatively open access to the Internet (which is recommended), it may mean that students will be drawn to other websites such as video gaming or television or movie streaming websites. This can utilize high levels of bandwidth, which can limit the performance of Internet-based activities that are more strictly academic. To strike the right balance of supporting student autonomy and providing good service and a reliably fast Internet for the learning environment, the IT staff will have to throttle traffic to highly visited, mostly nonacademic websites. A school should have a set up so that they can understand the Internet use of the school population and seek to improve service in a way that evolves as quickly as technology changes. For example, imagine the following situation: School IT staff at a school in the United States get a complaint from a teacher who says that while they are trying to Skype with a partner school in Costa Rica to discuss a biodiversity project that they are working on, the call keeps dropping, to the dismay of the students and teachers in both classrooms. The IT staff found that the time when this one particular teacher was teaching coincided with a period when a large number of students had their lunch break. Further investigation found that that particular hour had a huge amount of traffic on a video-streaming site. So while the students were watching television on their lunch break, students in the Spanish class were suffering as their Skype calls dropped or loaded painfully slowly. Schools can take a number of paths to solve this issue; one might be to block the TV-streaming site completely to give priority. Another school that places more value on student autonomy and community trust might consider throttling the speed of the video streaming site so that the experience is not as desirable for students. The essential consideration is that schools need to take into account many things when they are thinking about how to manage Internet access in their schools. And decisions about Internet connectivity can be complicated and sometimes nuanced, and all decisions will need to be based on the school community and norms of the culture of the school. Most importantly, those decisions should be made based on privileging students' and teachers' ability to collaborate and network their learning globally.

Accessibility

The example above leads us to the issue of access. Once teachers and students are connected to fast and reliable Internet connections, schools and school districts need to decide to what extent students and teachers will be able to use technology and connectivity on their own schedule to connect to others around the world. Many schools with Internet connectivity limit the websites that students (and in some cases teachers) are able to access during school hours and on the school campus. There are many services that schools can choose from to restrict the access to different categories of websites or specific websites. The ways that schools and districts use these services varies widely, from completely unfiltered Internet, to blocking categories like pornography, gambling, and social media. It might seem surprising to some that social media can be listed with websites associated with illicit and illegal activities, but in terms of discipline and social issues that arise in schools today, the bulk of issues with middle and high school students has to do with the use of social media.

Therefore, some of the most blocked websites are the social media sites most commonly used by the students at the school. This is a challenge for the school because if you want to connect students to the world and have them collaborating in virtual spaces (which we do!), then social media is one of the most effective ways to do this. There have been many efforts to pull students and teachers into "safer" websites that are designed purely for educational use but have similar looks and feel to popular social media sites. Still, even with so much attention to building course and learning management systems (CMS and LMS) that appeal to students in the same way that their social media site du jour does, the educational technology always seems to fall short of widespread engagement of interest of students. What schools should be doing is creating curriculum around building community norms and practices for using social media in public and responsible ways.

This work of engaging a community in dialog about the threats of the Internet can be valuable, and also very challenging. Many schools and teachers might have a sense that students need to be controlled and protected from the dangers lurking in the dark corners of the Internet. While there are real dangers that can emerge from an online presence, most of the harm that comes to teenagers online is from their peers.

In education, along with other fields, enthusiasm for the transformational power of the Internet on our society and education has been matched by fear of what our children and students might find—or how they might be found—in this electronic environment (Montgomery, 2010). There are several tiers of questions that relate to Internet filtering and monitoring of student Web traffic in school. First, there are legal questions: What is the school's responsibility? What are the actual laws and also case law precedent to which schools need to attend to not be at risk? Within those legal boundaries, there is a spectrum of practice that schools can consider, depending on what type of environment and culture they hope to cultivate in addition to the realities of their school, including supervision and student and family make-up (Jansen, 2010). Second, schools should consider philosophical and educational questions such as the following: How much should schools filter? What categories of content are concerning? Should the filter be employed as a way to support good time management for students by blocking sites on which students tend to spend lots of time? How should these questions be answered by curriculum?

Legal Considerations

Since 2000, the Children's Internet Protection Act has mandated that all K–12 schools must filter Internet content to protect children from harm and exposure to objectionable and age-inappropriate content. This filtering is a condition of one type of federal funding. There have been a number of attempts to change this law, most notably the *American Library Association vs. the United States,* which was filed in 2001 and settled by the Supreme Court in 2003. In this suit, the American Library Association (ALA) fought to defend the First Amendment in public and school libraries. Central to their argument was the concern about a digital divide among those children who had access to information from computers in their homes and those (primarily of lower socioeconomic status) who did not have access to that same information because their access was limited to that available at school (Jaeger, Bertot, & McClure, 2004).

The US Supreme Court upheld the law but emphasized that adult patrons of the libraries could have the filter lifted for "bona fide" research purposes. However, it does not define that term well (Jansen, 2010). Essentially, users have to justify their unfiltered search to a librarian who, if they see fit, should have the ability to lift the filter in a timely manner.

In 2006, there was an additional effort at legislation to block all social media sites called the "Deleting Online Predators Act." This act has been bouncing around the US House of Representatives and the Senate since its introduction. There is consensus that online predators are a danger to children, but there is lack of agreement on the tools that should be employed to limit their access to kids without having a detrimental impact on children's education. The ALA has taken a strong stance against this bill (Jaeger et al., 2004).

In order to foster an environment in which students have personalized connectivity to leverage the remarkable tools on the Internet to globalize their learning, schools need to review, reexamine, and in many cases revise their policies and practices of how students are able interact in online spaces.

Hardware

There are many resources available to schools exploring the choices around hardware for learning. Some schools, districts, and states have one-to-one laptop or tablet programs in which each student has a personal device. Some schools even have two-to-one programs in which students have a tablet and a laptop. These devices can be family owned or school owned and managed—there is no right or wrong answer for all schools in the world. There are certainly programs that cause less financial strain on the school but still provide access for students and teachers, like lab or cart set ups. Each school or district has to make a decision based on the reality in their school(s). The key is to ensure that the decisions made around issues of hardware take into consideration the core value that students and teachers must be able to leverage global resources on the Internet to do their work. This will manifest itself in different ways in different communities.

Plan for Globalness: Structures, Staffing, and Hiring

Lead Toward the Global Campus

If the transition from a traditional school to a global campus is a central part of somebody's job, then it is more likely to be a successful transition. In your school or district, it might be the superintendent or the principals who consider that part of their job, or it might be that schools should create a position that keeps a keen eye on the global education initiatives of the school. There are many ways in which the work of becoming a global campus is everyone's job, from the systems analyst in information technology, to the security guards who are versed in how to greet international educators coming to visit the school. One universal truism in education is that educators, at every level, are busy. Our lives are filled with the packed days and long nights at the kitchen table, grading papers, planning lessons, or continuing to care for those in our charge in all sorts of ways. Everyone who works in schools has the opportunity to work to create the global campus, but it is likely that it is not at the forefront of everyone's priority list every day.

At the very well-financed end of the spectrum, this may mean that there is a full-time position (or more than one) with a leadership position at the school supporting the global initiatives and advocating for the global perspective when there are decisions to be made. Depending on the type and structure of the school, this could be an element of an administrator's job, or it could be a rotating faculty position. A number of independent schools in the United States have appointed directors of global initiatives or global programs, and the job position varies widely from school to school. However, what it has in common is that the directors are constantly working to evolve the concept of their own particular global campus, through planning and coordinating and developing curriculum, travel opportunity, and exchanges.

Hire for Global Mindedness

As a school leader or a supervisor of some sort, the easiest way to develop a globally committed faculty is to hire one. In your job descriptions and desired qualifications, consider listing multilingualism—not necessarily because you are looking to hire world language teachers, but because someone who speaks more than one language fluently has a skillset that might be more effective at nurturing global connections. Also, think about broadening the audience of your job postings—in addition to posting openings on your own website, and your local or regional job banks, consider using international school firms or job boards to fill positions. Finding teachers with experience in other parts of the world and authorizing them to do all they can to build your global campus goes a long way to creating global learning environments for students.

Provide Professional Development for Teachers

It is essential to support teachers in their professional growth as they evolve into architects of the global campus. Whether you are a district or school administrator or a teacher, global schools have to focus on supporting the work of classroom teachers. Each school with a global commitment has to be figuring out how to support, engage, and challenge classroom teachers. It is not sufficient for a school leader to spend time traveling abroad and impose rigorous international curriculum; they must take the time required to help teachers understand the essential role of global connections in their work. For some teachers, who have already had the opportunity to develop strong global competencies themselves, or maybe have traveled and worked in other parts of the country or world, this comes naturally, but for others who have not had the opportunities that a school may be committed to offering its students, it is essential to carefully craft learning opportunities for educators.

There are many ways that schools can support professional development with a global perspective. Perhaps each time an administrator travels for a conference or to nurture global connections, at least one teacher joins on the trip and Skypes with his or her students from the destination. Because international travel can be so expensive, schools can be quick to dismiss requests to support teachers to travel abroad for conferences or other professional learning opportunities. One of the greatest professional experiences that teachers can have is to attend an educational conference in another part of the world. For U.S. schools, the international school associations are a wonderful resource. For example, in Central and South America, there is the annual TRI Association Conference (TRI Association, n.d), and in Southeast Asia, there is the East Asia

Regional Council of Schools (EARCOS, n.d.) Conference. These conferences and others around the world offer educators the dual benefit of connecting to educators in other parts of the world and also connecting with a local culture outside of their own. It may cost a little more than attending a regional conference in your part of the United States, but the distance toward the globalized campus is huge. At these conferences, networking with other teachers becomes an opportunity to develop cross-cultural collaborations for their classrooms, and even eating meals becomes an experience to develop their own cross cultural competencies—most importantly empathy and multiple perspectives.

STRATEGIES FOR BUILDING A GLOBAL CAMPUS

The strategies in this chapter will mostly fall at the school and district level, as that is where most of the decisions about infrastructure and costs are made in schools. However, even in the individual classroom, there are ways in which teachers can leverage the resources they have and make strides toward the vision of a global campus.

In the Classroom

Share and Disseminate Resources
About Travel and Study Abroad (Beginning)

Teachers can subscribe to listservs and explore opportunities for their students and colleagues. There are many organizations that exist to create opportunities for students and educators to travel abroad. The U.S. State Department sponsors study abroad programs that are either fully funded or quite affordable. Also, educators can apply for grants and fellowships to study abroad with a focus on improving or globalizing their curriculum. In order to highlight these ideas, use some tricks from the marketing sector. Perhaps you can connect with a popular student club and invite them to promote these opportunities through skits at assemblies or short videos to share on social media. Also, in some regions, representatives from the organizations that offer excellent study abroad opportunities will be thrilled to send representatives to school campuses to promote their programs and speak with students and families. (One word of caution: Prior to opening your doors to companies, ensure that there is financial access for your population of students—some study-abroad organizations are for-profit enterprises that have little interest in ensuring that students from diverse socioeconomic backgrounds have access to their programs. A quick question to them about financial aid, cost, and percentage of students receiving aid or scholarships should provide some good sense of where they stand.)

Just from sharing and promoting these opportunities that other organizations offer, students and teachers will take advantage of opportunities, return to the school, and further promote the experience of working globally. Over time, this simple (and cost-effective) act of sharing and promoting opportunities can make a real shift in the global mindset of the school climate.

In the School

Leverage Partnerships or
Outsource Information Technology Services

Some of the most significant costs associated with having a robust technology ecosystem in schools are not the hardware or even the infrastructure to support Internet connectivity, but the costs associated with the human resources required to make everything run smoothly. One of the most important elements of a strong and effective technology program in schools is staffing to make it all work smoothly and collaborate with teaching staff to ensure that the technology is meeting the evolving needs of the learners in the school or schools. An amazing IT staff will include an array of people who support upkeep and imaging and distribution of devices, people who manage data for the school, and people who have a strong technical background and the skills to work directly with teachers on integration. Few schools will have the financial resources to include all these individuals in their staff, so why not consider a job-sharing model?

Districts or even consortiums of private schools could develop a shared philosophy and vision for the technology integration and then establish a team of people to support different schools throughout the week. This consolidation of skills could be a real economic boon to a school. In addition, if there is the open-mindedness to have an instructional leader with strong technology skills leading or working in this team, it could increase cross-pollination between campuses, which is actually the first step in being able to become a global campus. If your school(s) or district is ready to explore this possibility, there will be some work to be done with legal and human resources, but there are models out there that schools can look to as starting points.

Create a Bring-Your-Own-Device (BYOD) Technology Program

Many schools have established a technology program based on students bringing their own devices to school. This is not a free ride for the school because the school still needs to provide Internet service, possible devices for teachers, and also make decisions about how they will support and train faculty and staff (and maybe students) and offer technology support. One main benefit of school-issued devices is uniformity in the ecosystem—everyone uses the same or similar devices, and the staff (and teaching faculty) is skilled at managing those devices. In a BYOD program, there can be greater variability, unless the school is specific about what devices it requires. The balancing tension here is that a BYOD model can offer greater student and family choice about the devices it uses and give students a sense that they are able to make decisions about the ways in which they most effectively interface with technology. The biggest issue in a BYOD program is equity. Schools need to take a careful look at ensuring that their technology program is not perpetuating the digital divide. Arrangements need to be made to ensure that students whose families do not have access to funding for computers or other devices get access.

Host Events and Performances for Visiting Groups

Depending on the location of your school, there may be the opportunity to welcome artists, scholars, or performance groups from other parts of the world as visitors to your class or school. Depending on the level of integration (class visits over days or weeks, versus a single afterschool event or performance), there can be a good deal of logistical organization involved in arranging these visits. Still, it is a great way for the school community to have access to people and ideas from other parts of the world. Ideally, each visit would involve question-and-answer or small-group discussion sessions with students, either with prepared questions or at least having done some prior research about the group or organization. Also, these visits can result in meaningful partners for future collaborations. For example, a performing group comes to the school, and then a month later, members of that group Skype with students from a class at the school, while the students share a short performance that they made, inspired by the visit. This would be a great way for students to integrate the global experience into their own learning and expression and then demonstrate that learning with a product for an authentic audience.

In the School System

Create a Global Programs Leadership Position

As suggested earlier in the chapter, one of the most efficient ways to move the concept of a global campus forward is to add that work into someone's job description. Some schools have established central offices of global initiatives in an effort to do this. This could be a school or a districtwide resource that meets the needs of the school(s) and moves projects forward as directed by the school and or district leadership. The job description would vary depending on the needs of the organization(s) that the position is supporting. In some schools, the director of this center might work closely with teachers on developing globally connected curriculum or projects. In another context, they might support planning of travel experiences integrated into credit-bearing courses. Also, this might be a position that coordinates with the technology integration team if the school(s) are keenly focused on developing partnerships and exchanges mediated by technology.

This leader or advocate of the Global Campus could be written into a new job description, or it could become part of a restructured job. If it is possible to make this position a part of the core leadership team, or to report regularly to that team, it will make the efforts more visible, and the needs associated with this work will be more likely to be met.

Welcome Visiting Teachers

Globally, there are many schools interested in having their school leadership, and teachers learn from other schools around the world. Your school(s) can think creatively about how to get teachers to join your team from other parts of the world. There are many challenges associated with this, and employing foreign nationals in the United States (schools or districts would have to have particular visa-granting status as approved by SEVIS), but there are many ways to invite global perspectives into your campus without having to grant J1 visas.

One way to globalize the faculty is to have teachers join the faculty sponsored by other organizations. There are a number of organizations that sponsor teachers, particularly in traditionally hard-to-staff world languages such as Mandarin Chinese or Arabic. Among the organizations that schools might look to are the Qatar Foundation and the Confucius Institute (n.d.), both of which have programs for supporting teachers in K–12 schools. These organizations handle all of the visa issues and also, in some cases, cover the costs associated with hiring the teacher. Usually these appointments are a year or less, which might not be ideal if you are trying to implement a long-term language program, but if your school is trying to get something off the ground and isn't sure how to start, this might be a good possibility.

Also, schools or districts could create educator exchange programs with partner schools. This would involve teachers making for short- or long-term visits to your school while still being employed at their home school. You could welcome them to visit classes, attend faculty and staff meetings and learn more about your school, perhaps while researching a theme that is of interest to their schools. Also, they could give guest speeches in classes and perhaps facilitate connections and projects with their home school. Just the presence and perspective of a visiting educator can do a great deal to broaden the global perspective of a school.

REFLECTION: WE CAN DO THIS!

Even schools with significant financial resources are not without limitations when it comes to realizing their goals of becoming a global campus. One of the most cost effective modes of meaningful global collaborations is through projects and exchanges mediated by technology. Therefore, our first order of business in schools needs to be ensuring that our students and faculty have connectivity and access—however we have defined that for our schools. Second is the focus on human resources—who we hire and how we deploy them in our schools is an essential issue. When hiring decisions are made with faculty, we can seek out candidates who have themselves demonstrated capacities that will be of value in nurturing the global campus—multilingualism, experience living, or extensive travel abroad. And finally, we will look to be opportunistic about the global opportunities that are available to our schools and communities at relatively low or no cost, such as subsidized visiting teacher programs, travel sponsored by organizations, or visiting performance groups. Added all together, our campuses will be well on their way to being globally connected in service of our students' learning without breaking the budget.

ACTIVITY #1: JOB DESCRIPTIONS FOR LEADING THE GLOBAL CAMPUS ADMINISTRATORS

Participants: Administrative team, including human resources staff

Objective: Too often in schools, we focus on hiring people with a very specific skillset, and we ignore some of the qualities that would be essential for developing a global campus. The purpose of this activity is to engage the people most likely to be writing job descriptions and doing hiring in schools to think about the qualities in new employees that they think would move the school or district most toward its aspirations of having a global campus.

Materials

- Computers, Internet access to share documents such as Google Docs

Procedure

Step 1 (20 minutes): In small groups (two to three people), start a shared Google Document and imagine that you are writing a job description for the director of global initiatives in your school or district. What should the desired qualifications be? What will the responsibilities be?

Step 2 (20 minutes): Have each group briefly share their work with the larger group.

Step 3 (10 minutes): Discussion: What do we notice about the job descriptions? What surprises us? What did we like about other groups' descriptions? What were the common themes? What might have been missing?

Step 4 (10 minutes): Each small group should now write two to six bullet points to include in every job description moving forward, particularly for teachers. If they are stuck, they can imagine that they had 300 applicants for every position? Or start with the prompt, "In a perfect world our candidates would be able to . . ." What are the qualifications that every new hire in our school (or school system) should have?

Step 5 (10 minutes): Share out bullet points and discuss which ones (if any) might be feasible to include in DQs for subsequent job positions in the school or district.

Activity #2: A Dream Global Professional Development Experience

Participants: Administrators and/or teachers

Objective: The purpose of this activity is to increase awareness about the possibility of global travel combined with professional development experiences. Even if there is no budget for global travel in the school, the activity will leave teachers and administrators with an expanded sense of their global learning community.

Materials

Internet access and digital tools for conducting Web searches

Process

Step 1: A Learning Journey (30–40 minutes)

Organize the group into pairs or groups of three and have them research professional conferences in regions of the country or world other than where your school is located. Invite the groups to plan a week-long professional development trip that includes school visitations, sightseeing, and some sort of professional event (conference or workshop).

Have the group prepare a rough budget and day-by-day itinerary. This is a quick activity, so things don't have to be too precise.

Step 2: Sharing Your Journeys
(30 minutes, depending on the size of the group)

Give each group 3 minutes to share their journey. If the gathering space has a projector, they may use three to five slides to enhance their sharing.

Next Steps

Invite the participating educators to make contact with a person that they might come across in their proposed learning journey. They can either try to connect with a teacher at one of the schools they thought of visiting or follow some presenters at the proposed conference on Twitter. Have individuals who accept this challenge share out what connections they made at the next meeting or gathering.

ACTIVITY #3: MAPPING OR GLOBAL REACH

Participants: School community

Objective: To increase schoolwide awareness of the global relationships at the school in order for the members of the community to begin to imagine themselves as a globally connected school.

Materials

- A wall-size map of the world (can be ordered online or have an art class make one)
- Pins or small flags

Process

Step 1

Each week, for a month or two, post a new sign by the map inviting people to pin locations based on the question asked:

- Post pins where your ancestors are from.
- Post a pin to the places in the world where you have traveled or lived in.
- Post a pin to the places in the world where you have friends living.
- Post a pin to the places in the world you have studied.
- Post a pin to the places in the world you would like to travel.

Take a picture of the map each week and publish it in school newsletters or other forms of communications. Invite all members of the school community to participate.

Reflection: Have teachers and/or students engage in discussion about how we could leverage all of our global connections and interests more directly in student learning.

REFERENCES

Center for Automotive Research. (2014). Just how high-tech is the automotive industry? Prepared for auto alliance. Retrieved from http://www.autoalliance.org/index.cfm?objectid=DED64A00-7C8F-11E3-9303000C296BA163

Confucius Institute. (n.d.). Retrieved from http://www.chinesecio.com/m/cio_wci

East Asia Regional Council of Schools Conferences. (n.d.). Retrieved from https://www.earcos.org/conf_calendar.php

Jaeger, P. T., Bertot, J. C., & McClure, C. R. (2004). The effects of the Children's Internet Protection Act (CIPA) in public libraries and its implications for research: A statistical, policy, and legal analysis. *Journal of the American Society for Information Science and Technology, 55*(13), 1131–1139. doi:10.1002/asi.20072

Jansen, B. (2010). Internet Filtering 2.0: Checking intellectual freedom and participative practice at the schoolhouse doors. *Knowledge Quest, 39*(1), 46–54.

McDonald, J. F. (2014). What happened to and in Detroit? *Urban Studies, 51*(16), 3309–3329. doi:10.1177/0042098013519505

Montgomery, B. (2010). Generation digital: Politics, commerce, and childhood in the age of the Internet. *International Journal of Applied Psychoanalytic Studies, 7*(1), 94–98. doi:10.1002/aps

Oxford Community Schools, Michigan. (n.d.). Retrieved from http://www.oxfordschools.org/

Qatar Foundation International grants. (n.d.). Retrieved from http://qfi.org/grants/

TRI Association: Association of American Schools Conference. (n.d.). Retrieved from http://www.tri-association.org/page.cfm?p=1

Index

Note: In page references, f indicates figures.

CORWIN
A SAGE Publishing Company

Helping educators make the greatest impact

CORWIN HAS ONE MISSION: to enhance education through intentional professional learning.

We build long-term relationships with our authors, educators, clients, and associations who partner with us to develop and continuously improve the best evidence-based practices that establish and support lifelong learning.

Solutions you want. Experts you trust. Results you need.

AUTHOR CONSULTING

Author Consulting

On-site professional learning with sustainable results! Let us help you design a professional learning plan to meet the unique needs of your school or district. www.corwin.com/pd

INSTITUTES

Institutes

Corwin Institutes provide collaborative learning experiences that equip your team with tools and action plans ready for immediate implementation. www.corwin.com/institutes

ECOURSES

eCourses

Practical, flexible online professional learning designed to let you go at your own pace. www.corwin.com/ecourses

READ2EARN

Read2Earn

Did you know you can earn graduate credit for reading this book? Find out how: www.corwin.com/read2earn

Contact an account manager at (800) 831-6640 or visit **www.corwin.com** for more information.